Barton Publishing presents

One Sister Away:

Encouraging Words From One Sister to Another

Compiled by: Cheryl Barton

Barton Publishing, LLC
P.O. Box 962
Reisterstown, Maryland 21136
www.bartonpublishingLLC.com
Phone: 443-379-3612

Scripture quotations are taken from the Holy Bible, New International Version ®, Copyright© 1984 by the International Bible Society, Used by Permission of Zondervan Publishing House. All Rights Reserved.

Scripture quotations are taken from The Holy Bible, The Message, Copyright © by Eugene H. Peterson 1993, 1994, 1995, 1996, 2000, 2001, 2002. Used by permission of Tyndale House Publishers, Inc.

Scripture quotations in this publication are from the Contemporary English Version Copyright © 1991, 1992, 1995 by American Bible Society. Used by Permission.

Scripture quotations in this publication are from the King James Version and authorized by King James Version

No part of this publication may be reproduced, stored in a retrieval system, or transmitted in any form or by any means, including, but not limited to electronically, mechanical recording or photocopying without prior written permission of the publisher. For permission requests, write to the publisher, addressed "Attention: Permissions Coordinator," at the address above.

Ordering Information:
Quantity sales: Special discounts are available on quantity purchases by corporations, associations and others. For details, contact the publisher at the address above.

Copyright © 2014 Barton Publishing, LLC
All rights reserved.

ISBN: 0692301151
ISBN-13: 978-0692301159

Table of Contents

Dedication
Acknowledgements

"We Are Our Sister's Keeper"	Cheryl Barton
"Tea Time With La - May I Suggest?"	LaTonya Summerville
"All I Want"	Michelle Russell
"Don't Be a Mean Girl"	Kaylani Thomas
"I'm a Boss"	Cheryl Barton
"The Ultimate Girl Talk"	Chynae Barton
"Forgiveness"	Mia Minion
"I Am Still Standing"	Sandra L. Fletcher
"We're In This Together"	Teresa Graves
"No Matter What"	Kimberly P. Carter
"Inextinguishable Lights"	Barbara Barton
"Who Are They?"	Cheryl Barton
"Emmanuel Come Down"	Michelle Russell
"No Regrets"	LaTonya Summerville
"Party of One"	Jaye Matthews
"But Still I Stand"	Geezie Reaves
"My Fantasy"	Michelle Russell
"Two Worlds, One Girl"	Laniece Oliver
"Once There Were Three"	Cheryl Barton
"God Cares"	Mary J. Demory
"Purpose From My Pain"	Wonda Oliver
"Our Littles"	LaTonya Summerville
"God Is In Control"	Irishteen Thomas
"Compassion Flowing From My Heart to Your Heart"	Dr. Simone Gibson
"I Can, You Can"	Susie Lang
"Try Again"	Cheryl Barton
"What's For Me"	Michelle Russell

DEDICATION

This book is dedicated to every sister who struggles daily to be seen and heard. We see you, we hear you and we're here for you. Never give up!

ACKNOWLEDGMENTS

If you believe that all you are capable of is what you're already doing, you are doing a disservice to yourself and those around you. Give thanks for the gifts and talents you have and use them to see how far and how wide you can expand your reach. The possibilities are endless.
– Cheryl Barton

I want to thank everyone who accepted the call and agreed to be a part of this project to reach out and embrace another sister through the pages of this book. My first thought with this project was how awesome it would be to get others to join me in my desire to inspire and motivate another sister with love and encouragement. Sometimes we get so caught up in all of the things that keep us busy that we forget to take the time to let another sister know that we have her back. I thank each of you from my heart. I could not have done this without you. You each inspire me. *Cheryl*

AVAILABLE FROM BARTON PUBLISHING:

'DOWN, BUT NOT OUT: BREAKING CHAINS'

Dana Carr believed she had the perfect marriage until her husband of seventeen years moved out declaring he needed space. She'd spent her life making her family her one and only priority, forgetting about her own goals and desires. A chance meeting with handsome stranger, Hunter Gray, opens her eyes to what's been missing in her life; being cherished like a woman should, unconditionally.

Terri Bryant thought she had to have a man who was older and successful in order to find the kind of love she desired, even if she had to deal with being mistreated and disrespected. Into her life walks a much younger man, Kerrion Lee, who she thought didn't measure up to her standards. She's caught off guard when he shows her that his age and status have nothing to do with showing her the respect she deserves by helping her see her true self-worth.

Karina Joseph can't let go of the past that has set the tone for her present, leading into a bleak future. She's a young mother of two, living in the hood and finding the only way to survive is to use her body to get what she wants, even if it means attracting some of the seediest men around. A minor run in with a car and its driver, Dr. Mykel Tanner, puts her on a new path to independence, a better outlook on life and a man she never thought would be within her reach.

The determination of each woman to discover who she is and who she can become is proof that you can't hold a good woman down once she finds her true self-worth. Despite each of their downfalls with the wrong man, they find that the love and support of the *RIGHT* man proves that they may have been down, but they shouldn't be counted out.

Get 'Down, But Not Out: Breaking Chains' and other projects from Barton Publishing at www.bartonpublishingLLC.com.

~SISTERHOOD~

We Are Our Sister's Keeper
By Cheryl Barton

Who said you didn't matter?
We as a society put too much stock in other's opinions of us and those opinions may have made you question who you are and what your purpose in life may be. There will always be people who will have something to say about you and some will do it just to bring you down. There comes a time when you have to encourage yourself and know that you were created to be different. If we were all made the same, we would be faced with looking at a mirror image of ourselves every day and that, I believe, would be a boring existence. Maybe at this point in your life you haven't discovered exactly what you're supposed to do, but I'm declaring today, don't give up and never give in to thoughts that you don't matter. Remember, you matter to me and there is someone who is counting on you to matter to them.
I am My Sister's Keeper!

Who said you wouldn't make it?
Opportunity is just an arms-length away; reach out and grab it. If you're feeling a little down and need a boost, look back and call my name and use my shoulders to stand on. We are all given one life and every moment of it should be spent leaving the bad in the past, happy that the present is an opportunity to try again and thankful when the future presents itself as a clean, fresh and new slate to be formed into whatever we want it to be, keeping our dreams alive. I believe in you and I know that only greatness lies ahead of

you. It's a greatness that can't be stopped.
I am My Sister's Keeper!

Who claimed you weren't pretty enough?
Let your mirror be a reflection of what you see and not what others tell you they see. I have always believed that beauty is in the eyes of the beholder and that first starts with a look at you from your own perspective. Who is the authority over what is and is not beautiful? When it comes to you, you are. That sight you see is who you are supposed to be and if you happen to see a flaw and want to do something about it, do it because it's what you want to do and not because someone says what they see doesn't work for them. You are beautiful and if you've never heard those words spoken to you before, start with saying them out loud to yourself. YOU ARE BEAUTIFUL!
I am My Sister's Keeper!

Who silenced you as if your words didn't matter?
There are those in this world who can't hear or speak and that's beyond their control. If you have the ability to do both, be thankful and know that your words can be used to help, heal and soothe. Remember words can also be used to hurt, harm and destroy so be careful of the words you choose and remember what you put out, you may get back. Which will you choose? In a world where everything is getting louder and faster and those who are slower and quieter may be left unseen and unheard, but even if you have to shout it out to the world, let people know you are here and what you

have to say matters. Take the time to speak life into yourself and then do so into those around you. You may never get a thank you, but the sweet sound of your voice may never inspire and encourage if you let anyone silence you. Speak up and speak out! If no one else is listening, I am.
I am My Sister's Keeper!

Let's come together and prove we're not always competing with each other, we're not tearing each other down or working to keep each other from being successful.

Let's together make the letters of the word "SISTER" stand for "*S*isters *I*n *S*ync *T*o *E*levate *R*elevance".

We all matter and We Are Our Sister's Keeper!

~FRIENDSHIP~

Tea Time With La – May I Suggest?
By LaTonya Summerville

Supporting someone is not handicapping them to continue the quest in ignorance. Strategically and tactfully let them know that they are WRONG!

Don't give someone so much that you overdraft your happiness and livelihood. Lord knows they'll take it.

Deliberately be obsessed in your quest for strengthening your weakest skill (relationships, finances, career...). Whatever it is don't give up!

There is always more to the story...that's it.

Settle it by uncovering the root of the problem; there is always a common denominator in a repetitive ruckus!

Everyone deserves a chance; Lord knows I've had more than I can count.

Take the step and a half from in front of brother and sister as well as the step out of mother and father; it makes the love step-half! No worries you'll get it later.

Prayer does change things - when you act on it.

Our souls are much smarter than our bodies; it departs from things and people that aren't good for us at the moment of discernment. While our bodies decides to stick with it and later wonder why does it hurt so bad, the little voice you've been hearing is your soul saying "drop that zero".

Be a good friend and tell them to suck it up and take responsibility for their own actions!

.

~LOVE~

All I Want
By Michelle Russell

I want mountains, I want birds
I want butterflies and bees
I want a special place for special times
I want you, my love by the sea
I want more today than we had yesterday
I want chowder from shiny spoons
I want our union to beam at midnight
Like the sun through our room at noon.

When all my wants are wants no more
When God has given all we've asked for
We'll be eating shellfish by the bay
And I'll whisper in a most loving way
I have you, you have me
We've both become what we wanted to be
We've donned smiles, we've shed tears
With God we're together all these years.

So many nights at your rib during thunder
You were always up when I was under
If we part, know it is God's will
Just remember this love is still
I want clear, clear skies
I want less, less tears
I want poetry in song
I want love, I want liberty
I want what I've had all along.

~LEADER~

Don't Be a Mean Girl
By Kaylani Thomas

My daddy says children are not born mean. He says they get it from the people around them. They hear mean things that grown-ups say and they repeat them because they want to be like them.

One day in my neighborhood I was playing with my friends and a new girl who moved near us came out to play. I was ready to play with her, but my other friends said no. They said I shouldn't play with her because they only wanted us to be friends and not be friends with anyone else. At first I didn't see anything wrong with having the same friends I already had, but I didn't understand why we shouldn't make new friends with the new girl. She could be our friend too.

The new little girl was very nice and friendly and came over to us and told us her name. She had a very pretty name and I liked it. I was going to tell her my name when one of my other friends said don't tell her our names because we don't like her and don't want to be her friend. I did what everyone else did and walked away from the new little girl. When I turned around I could see that she was sad and I felt really bad about that. I asked my friends why did we do that and they said because we don't like new people and because new people would join us and try to make us not be friends anymore. I asked them how did they know that and one said because she heard her mother say to some of her friends that she didn't like a new lady at work even though she didn't know her and that she was too old to try and make new friends so she didn't speak to her when the new lady tried to be nice and friendly. I asked her why would her mother do that and she said she didn't know. She just knew that new people didn't have any friends, so why should they want to be friends with someone who didn't have any friends.

We played for the rest of the afternoon until my daddy called me inside. After I went inside I could still see the new little girl sitting on her step playing with her doll by herself and she looked sad when she looked at the other girls playing and not liking her. I felt really sad for the new little girl and didn't believe she didn't have any friends and I didn't like that I let my friends make me be mean to a little girl who was pretty and friendly.

While my daddy fixed me a snack I told him what happened with the new little girl. He went from smiling to not being very happy. He asked me why I didn't tell the new little girl my name when she told me her name. I didn't know what to say because I didn't know why I acted like that.

He said, "Kaylani, you know better than to be rude to anyone, especially another little girl who was looking for a friend."

I was even sadder then. My daddy asked me what else happened after we walked away. I told him we played some other games. He asked me did I have fun and I said yes. He asked me if the other little girl looked like she was having fun playing by herself and I said no, she looked very sad playing all alone.

I then told him that one of my friends started calling the

new little girl mean names and they said them loud to her and then we all laughed. My daddy wanted to know why did I laugh and did I think it was funny. I told him no I didn't think it was funny, but I laughed because I was told to laugh and everyone else laughed. We wanted to let her know that we didn't want to be her friend so we talked about her. I was about to reach for my snack when my daddy pulled it back and asked me if I thought I deserved a snack and I said yes because it was my favorite, macaroni and cheese in the blue and orange bowl. My daddy looked at me sad and that made me even sadder. My daddy never gets mad at me or looks at me sad, but today he was sad because I was a mean girl.

My daddy explained to me it's not nice being mean to someone especially when you don't know them or even have a reason to be mean to them. He's always taught me to be nice and pleasant and to be a leader, not a follower. Was I being a leader or a follower? I wasn't being a leader and he didn't like that. He wanted to know how I would feel if children treated me like that when we moved into the neighborhood. I told him I would be sad. He sent me to my room to think about how I could have been nicer to the new little girl in the neighborhood.

I went to my room and I cried. At first I cried because I didn't get my snack and I really wanted it. Then I knew my daddy was right. I was a mean girl and he doesn't want me to be like that. He and my mommy are always nice to people. I went into my daddy's room to look out of the window again and I still saw the little girl sitting on her step by herself watching all of the other children playing. I was sad for her because we were mean to her and I was sad for me because I didn't like how I treated her made me feel. She looked sad and lonely and I was in the house, without my snack now sad and lonely too.

I went back to the kitchen and told my daddy I was sorry for what I did and that it wasn't right for me to be mean to the new little girl because other children wanted to be mean to her. He asked me what I thought I should do and I told him I wanted to go say that I was sorry and ask if she wanted to play with me. When my daddy smiled, I knew it was the right thing to do. My daddy had a good idea. He said he would walk over to the new girl's house with me so that he could say hello to her parents and then I could say hello to the new little girl.

We walked out of our house and went straight to her house. My daddy asked her if her mommy or daddy were home and when she said yes, he asked her to get them so that he could say hello.

When she went inside of her house I saw my other friends looking at my daddy and me. The new little girl came back with her mommy and daddy. My daddy told them his name and my name and the new little girl's mom told us their names. While my daddy talked to her mom and dad, I said hello to the new little girl and she smiled at me. She said my name was very pretty and she had never heard a name like mine before. I told her my mommy said my name was from Hawaii where she met my daddy. We sat down on her step and I asked her if she liked school. We kept talking until my daddy said it was time to go and then I was again sad. I was having a lot of fun talking to my new friend. My daddy said I would be able to play with her again soon.

The next day my other friends asked me what I was doing over at the "ugly girl's" house. I didn't like what they said because the new little girl was not ugly and she was very nice. I did what my daddy told me to do and I told them it wasn't nice to be mean. I told them I didn't want to be a mean girl and that the new little girl was really nice and so was her mom and dad. I told them she liked to read like me and like me she was going to get a new bike for her birthday and we were going to ride them together to the playground across from our houses. I told them that having new friends was not a bad thing and just because someone was new it didn't mean they didn't have any friends because now she had a new friend and it was me and that they could be friends with her if they wanted to. I told them I was going to be her friend even if they didn't want to, but I didn't understand why they wanted to be mean for no reason. They didn't know either and asked if I thought the new little girl would want to be friends with them too. I said I think we should all be friends with her and tell her we were sorry for saying mean things to her.

We walked over to her house and asked if she could come outside to play. When she came out we all said our names and said we were sorry for being mean to her and she smiled.

We all played together the whole summer and now I have a new best friend. I was excited the first day of school to see that she was going to the same school and we rode the school bus together. My new best friend and her family are very nice people and because we are friends, our mommies and daddies are friends and when my mommy and daddy had friends over, they invited my new best friend and her mom and dad and we played until we fell asleep. We are now taking karate classes together near our house and we are forever best friends.

It's not nice being mean to someone and you don't know them. Like my daddy said, children are not born mean; they get it from the people around them. Grown-ups should watch what they say around children because children do what they see their parents and other grown-ups doing and if it's not something nice, the children will grow up from being mean children to mean adults and that would be sad.

~POWER~

I'm a Boss!
By Cheryl Barton

I may be small in stature, but I'm large in my thoughts
Because I'm a Boss!

I may not speak up or out loudly, but what I have to say
is worthy of your ear
Because I'm a Boss!

My steps may be slow, but the imprint I'm leaving in the
sand speaks volumes
Because I'm a Boss!

My car may not be shiny or new, but my ride takes me to
my purpose
Because I'm a Boss!

The house I call a home doesn't have the most expensive
designer furniture, but it's clean and it's mine
Because I'm a Boss!

My clothes aren't designer and they may not turn heads,
but they keep me warm and they cover all the important
parts to God's liking
Because I'm a Boss!

The job I go to every day won't make me a millionaire,
but I'm rich in love, family and life and that makes going to
work well worth it
Because I'm a Boss!

The love I have to give may not move mountains or have
men dropping at my feet because I'm the greatest, but my
love can heal a wounded heart, mend a broken spirit and

bind up what someone else may have torn down
Because I'm a Boss!

I fell, I crawled, I struggled to stand, but I looked up and I saw a sister who offered me a helping hand. Now I stand, I walk and I run with enthusiasm and purpose
Because I'm a Boss!

I'm not perfect or on the "A" list, but with my Boss mentality, my head is held high because I know that the prospects of my tomorrow being brand new and full of break-throughs are in my favor.

With my Boss mindset, I'm already on my way to being large and in charge.
Because I'm a Boss!

~EDUCATE~

The Ultimate Girl Talk: From One Queen to Another
By Chynae V. Barton

Hey my beautiful sisters! I know many of you are living in that stage of your life where you are preparing to go to college in the next few years. I have been in the same spot where you all are now, so I'm here to let you in on a few secrets that they don't teach you in high school to prepare you for the "real" college experience.

The four years that you are in high school can either make or break you when it comes to preparing for your future. Many young people think it's fun and cute to play around and not do what they need to do in order to ensure that they will have a good future once they leave high school. Here are some things that I wish an older girl had shared with me when I first entered high school.

High School –

High school is not a huge indoor playground. It is not okay to ever skip class for any reason. If you do not have a legit reason for not going to class, then you need to go and remember peer pressure won't last forever and your future, determined by you starts now! If you start a bad habit of not going to class in high school, that will carry over into your college life and that could cause you to fail a class. If you miss three or more classes without a legitimate excuse, your teacher will fail you and not think twice about it. Just like you're there to get an education, the teachers are there to do their job, so don't expect any special treatment. They are preparing you for what the real world will be like, not to cater to you.

Another thing to be aware of is making sure your teachers know who you are and make a good impression on them. You never know when you'll need a recommendation from one of them for a job or even to get into college. It's always good to build a strong connection with people that you come into contact with because you never know how your connection with them can help you in the future.

When you do get to college (notice I didn't say if, but when you get to college) get to know your teachers and go to their office hours which is like the equivalent to coach class in high school. A professor, when you get to college, offers office hours for students so that they can express any concerns or problems that they may have about the class or any assignments that they may be having trouble with. Don't go through the semester being lost and making things hard for yourself. Use all of the resources that are given to you. Start thinking about this while in high school and connect with your teachers and ask if they have office hours. Learn to use your resources early.

Being the class clown is never the answer for trying to make friends or gain attention from anyone. That reputation of being a "bad girl" will follow you throughout high school and will also carry over into your college life. Remember, bad habits are hard to break. Everybody may be laughing with you when you're acting up, but they're also the ones turning in their work on time and attending every class. Don't assume that their involvement in your jokes and playing around means that they're slacking in the areas where they need to handle their business. You'll be the one ending up in trouble, whether it be a phone call home, being written up to your administrator or even going as far as you getting detention or being expelled. All of these things will shed a bad light on you as a student. Be on your best behavior at all times and if you feel the need or want to joke around, do it before and after school and not during when your classes are the stepping stone to your successful tomorrow.

College –

In high school, nearly everything is free or at a very low cost. Appreciate the fact that you get free or reduced lunch, the free textbooks, the field trips and other fun activities. Writing in the textbooks or ripping them up may seem fun while you're in high school, but once you get to college and you see that all the books you need in one semester can cost you up to and well over five hundred dollars, you'll treat those books with care so that you will be able to sell them back for a few extra dollars every semester.

As for those college textbooks, don't assume that you need the newest edition every year. There are websites like bookholders.com, chegg.com, and even amazon.com where you can buy the textbook you need for cheap prices and not burning a hole in your pocket or your parents' pockets. There are also e-book (kindle, nook, etc.) versions of textbooks available so look into that as well. Appreciate everything that you have now because nothing in college is free like that free ride most get in high school.

There's a time to party and there's a time to study. If you know that you have a test in the morning, it's not the end of the world if you stay in your room or in the library and study instead of going to 'turn up' with your friends. You'll find that you're paying ten dollars to go and party with the same people you see every day, listen to the same music you listen to every day and party at the same club every week. There's a party either on campus or off campus every other night so if you miss a few, you won't be missing out on a lot. Schoolwork always comes first, before any student organizations that you may join or and party that you think will be the move of the year. Every party is going to be advertised as the party of the year, so don't believe the hype. Study as much as you need to and make sure all of your work is completed and turned in on time and then you'll be surprised how much free time you'll have left over to party.

The college life is not strictly based around school work, and then you graduate with your degree and move on. Take time and get to know people. Networking is one of the greatest things you can do in college. Attend campus events and join different student organizations. You may not like every one that you join, so find out where you fit in and feel comfortable and stick with it.

Don't just stay in your room and not socialize. You can't fully enjoy the college experience if you don't get out and enjoy it and meet people. You don't have to become friends with every one you meet because gradually you'll get to know people and you'll be able to see who you really vibe with and who you don't.

Having a roommate may be a new experience for most of you if you choose to live on campus. If you can room with a friend, then do so, but make sure that you and your friend have similar living styles and standards. Sometimes rooming with friends may seem like a good idea until they start getting too comfortable and then you become uncomfortable. Whether you end up rooming with a friend or not, make sure that some rules and guidelines are established once you both are settled in your new place. You both have to share one space, so make sure you're both comfortable and respect each other's personal space.

If you end up not really connecting with your roommate, make sure you're still cordial and realize you don't necessarily have to be friends. Be nice and respectful and speak when you enter the room so that you don't make the situation awkward. If you have a problem with them, they won't know unless you say something, but don't approach them in an attacking kind of way. If the conversation gets volatile, contact your resident advisor and have them handle the situation. They may even help you find another roommate who you'd get along with. You don't want an uncomfortable situation to elevate to an unhealthy or unsafe situation. Settle things the right way and bring in the right people on staff to assist. Don't try to handle hostile situations by yourself. You pay to live there just like they do so don't feel that you have to be stuck living in a situation that you don't like. College years should be enjoyable and not full of frustration, anger or disrespect. Handle problems early and with civility.

On Your Own – Not! –

So you're finally on your own after eighteen years with

little to no parental guidance. All of a sudden you don't have a curfew and you have the freedom to act and dress how you'd like. Make sure you never forget that even when your family isn't around, you still have to represent them the same way that you would as if they were right there in your presence every day. You never know who you'll run into when you're out with your friends when you "think" no one is watching you the things that you do. Don't take the risk and continue to conduct yourself as the respectable young lady that your family raised you to be and then you won't have to worry about who's watching you and it saves you as well as your family unnecessary embarrassment.

Family is Everything –

Your family is the greatest set of people on this earth that you will ever encounter. Treasure them and respect them at all times because they only want the best for you. If you were to lose your parents today, do you really think the last argument you had with them about you being out late or getting in trouble in school was worth it? God put you in your family for a reason, so never take them for granted.

When you get to college, you will go from seeing your family every day to seeing them a few times a year and that will definitely make you appreciate them more.

Never think that just because your parent yells at you, that means they don't love you or care about you. If anything, it means that they love and care about you more than you could ever know or understand until you have your own children one day. When they're upset, give them some time to think about what happened and then you will be able to have a family discussion once they're not upset anymore and you can get past whatever incident may have occurred. Never hold a grudge against a member of your family because waking up in the morning is never guaranteed for anybody on this earth, so tell them you love them every chance you get. Never put a relationship or friendship before your family because when those people walk away, your family will always be there.

Love –

Love is a powerful thing, especially at a young age. You may think it's the best feeling in the world. Well, I'm here to tell you that every boy that tells you he loves you actually doesn't. He may love what you can do for him, but don't think that he is truly in love with you. Getting into serious relationships at a young age is something that most people in high school are not emotionally and mentally mature enough to deal with. These relationships can cause you to alienate yourself from your family and friends and can cause you to start acting differently and not always in a good way.

If a boy ever puts his hands on you he does not love you. If this ever happens, not only should you leave him, but you should tell an adult that you trust. If a boy is dating you and multiple females at one time, he does not love you. If a boy tries to tear you down emotionally, mentally, and spiritually just to keep you from building relationships and bonds with other people, he does not love you. Wait for the one guy who will love you unconditionally and puts your needs before his own. Wait for the guy that doesn't try to change you because he can see that you are a queen and isn't intimidated by your beauty and power.

Take your teenage and young adult years to discover who you truly are and what you want out of life before jumping into any serious relationships. You need to discover your own likes and dislikes before you can even attempt to make someone else happy.

It's okay to be by yourself sometimes. If you can't stand to be by yourself, what makes you think that someone else would want to be with you? Love yourself first before allowing someone to define what love is for you. If you love yourself, anyone coming into your life with expressions of love will be an enhancement because you're already filled with love and that will then have love overflowing all around you. Make friends, have fun, travel, discover new genres of music, join clubs at school and learn to love life.

Self-Esteem –

Self-esteem is something that a lot of young girls struggle with, mainly during their teenage years. First, let me say that no matter who you are, where you come from or what you have been through, you are a powerful, beautiful young lady who deserves the best of everything in life.

Never think that anyone else is better than you because that will hinder you from doing many great things that you think you may not be able to do. Never compare yourself to another person just because they may have something you want. You don't know what they went through to get it. Everyone on this earth has something about themselves that they are struggling with, even the most established celebrities that you see on television and in movies. They don't have it all together and they have not perfectly dotted every "I" or crossed every "T". Don't let the media fool you because celebrities are just regular people like you and me; they just happen to have the money to portray themselves the way they want the world to see them. You can use other people's success to motivate you, but never think that you're not worthy of being just as happy and successful in life.

It doesn't matter if you're a size two or a size twenty-two, you are beautiful. If you want to gain or lose weight that's nobody's business, but your own. Never change yourself for anyone else because at the end of the day, the way you look only affects you. Don't determine how beautiful you are based on society's standards because nobody in society truly likes everything about themselves. Sometimes they try to tear other people's physical attributes down because they aren't satisfied with their own self-image. It doesn't matter if you are light skin, brown skin, or dark skin you are just as beautiful as anyone else. Whether your hair is natural, permed, in braids, or in a weave, you are just as beautiful as anyone else. If you choose to wear no makeup or a face full of makeup, that's quite alright. As long as you look in the mirror and like what you see, don't worry about what anybody else thinks about you or what they have to say about you.

Chin Up –

You will go through some situations during your teenage years that you may not be feel you are able to handle or deal with. You can do anything you set your mind to. A bad situation or circumstance is not the end of the world for you.

You will always be destined for greater no matter where you come from or what you're going through. Whenever you're facing a tough situation, just remember that there are always people out here going through worse things than you or they may not have even woken up one morning, so always thank God for a new day, even if it's not one of your best.

Never give up on your dreams and goals. If you ever feel like you've gone as far as you possibly can, that means your goals aren't big enough. Always strive for the best of everything for yourself because you deserve it simply because you are a queen. Every morning when you wake up tell yourself "I am a beautiful, powerful woman of God and I can be who I want to be and do what I want to do." A good statement that my grandmother has instilled in my brain is "Who I am to be is up to me." The day she told me that for the first time was the day that I decided I was going to be something great and I wasn't going to let anyone or anything get in my way. Every time I hit a roadblock in my life or come across a situation that may have discouraged me in the past, I just say that statement in my head and I know that I'm going to be okay.

Be Heard –

Your voice is your most powerful weapon. Never let anyone silence you because your opinion is a reflection of your freedom to think for yourself. It's also a reflection of your own morals and values and that's something that no one on this earth can take away from you. Stand firm in who you are and always walk in your own truth. Be aware of the things you say to and about people because you never know how your words will affect someone else. Never tear down someone else to build yourself up. Always share kind words with someone you may or may not know because you never know what a person is going through. Maybe that person needs a little encouragement just to help them get through the day.

Never throw salt on or curse anyone's name and always help your sister's light shine at all times. When I use the term sister, I don't mean just your biological sister, but every female on this earth is your sister. Nobody can live on this earth alone and everybody needs a support system and someone that they can confide in and trust. That's what sisters are for.

Sisterhood –

My sister, I hope that when you enter college you will remember the advice that I have shared with you. It's my hope and prayer that all of my fellow sisters succeed in whatever paths you choose to take in this life. You only get one life to live, so never miss an opportunity to do something great. If you find something that you love to do, stick with it and always find ways to better perfect your crafts and talents. Remember that God is always in control of everything, so if you ever feel overwhelmed by a situation, put it in God's hands and watch Him work things out in your favor. Never forget that you are beautiful and always have the utmost respect for yourself so that no one would ever dream of disrespecting you.

My sister, I love you and you will do great things. Share an encouraging word with another sister today. Being a blessing to other people not only gives you a good feeling, but it's also very rewarding. What you put out into the universe is what you get back so always put out a good energy and you'll live a long and fulfilling life.

~FAMILY~

Forgiveness
By Mia Minion

How many people have you forgiven in your lifetime? What did they do to you? You've heard that old adage that you should forgive someone so that you can free yourself. You know – that boyfriend that did you wrong or that girlfriend that slept with your man. You can forgive that, right? How about forgiving a family member? Can you forgive your older brother or sister for bullying you all your life? That's pretty easy, right? How about a parent? Can you forgive your dad for abandoning you as a child? Yes, that's pretty straightforward too. I forgave my dad before he passed away and it felt pretty good.

Now I've listed a few scenarios that most people can relate to, but there is one scenario that I will bet would be difficult for the average person. How about forgiving your mom for being in your life? Yes, you heard me correctly. Forgive your mom for being in your life and making it what it was. Still confusing to you? Well, let me break it down for you. I had to forgive my mom for being who she was as a mother to me in order to be the daughter that I needed to be for her. Let me take you there.

It was Spring 2002 and I was at work when I got the call, "Mom is in the hospital and we don't know what's wrong with her." What?!! I froze. My mother has never been sick a day in her life. She's had some minor surgeries and a knee replacement, but that was pretty much it. I've actually never seen my mom sick; not even a cold. I left work in a panic and rushed to the hospital where she was with my head racing with thoughts of what happened. Did she have a stroke? A heart attack? Did she fall down and hurt herself? She was seventy-seven so all of these things could have happened. When I finally got to the hospital, she was propped up in bed in the triage area looking normal. There were no visible signs of trauma and she was talking normal. She said she was at the bank and lost the feeling in her leg and couldn't walk. That sounds like a stroke, but it was just her left leg and nothing else. Everything else was working fine. What?! What the hell does that mean?! Well, long story short, she no longer could walk and had to be cared for. This is where the forgiveness begins.

Let me start by saying my mother was not the typical mom. She worked nights and slept during the day so I hardly ever saw her except on the weekends. How can that be? She has children to raise. How can she be sleep? Well, it happened. My whole life as a child, my mother worked nights and slept during the day. When I came home from school the house was quiet. There was food prepared, but that was pretty much it. She never came to a Parent/Teacher Association meeting, a track meet, a basketball game, a volleyball game, nothing. I even graduated from Junior High School by myself.

I remember putting on my dress, walking up to the school and sitting in the auditorium, graduating, getting my certificate and then walking back home. Where was my Mom? Sleep. I remember my Senior Day in High School. We had a farewell day and I put on a dress. I won all kinds of awards because I was pretty smart and athletic. Where was my Mom? Sleep. I graduated from High School and my mom was there, but she didn't stay long. I don't know why.

My mother and I were not very close when I was growing up. I don't know why. She never showed me any affection. She never hugged me. She never said she loved me. She never comforted me when I was hurt. We never did anything together. She was never there for me growing up. I was alone. I had a mother, but at the same time, I didn't. She didn't tell me the things that a mother should tell a daughter like what happens when your period starts or anything about sex. I learned about that from sex education when it was okay to teach it in school. I never had a training bra. I just wore tight t-shirts under my shirts so that my breasts were smashed. When I finally got one, I wore it so much that it turned brown. It started off as white. She never combed my hair. I went to the hair salon every week to get my hair pressed and curled. I was never taught to be a lady. I grew up around my brothers and I acted like them. I was a tomboy. I was teased and tormented because I didn't know how to be a girl. Some people thought I was going to be gay. It's accepted now, but when I was growing up, it wasn't.

You might be thinking this is not so bad. At least you had a mother. Well, I beg to differ. It is one thing to have a mother, but it's a total different situation when you have a mother that cannot show you affection and looks at you like you are disgusting to her. That's right; my mother said I was disgusting and ugly. Yes, my mother said that to me! The funny thing was I look just like my mother. Did she think she was ugly? For the record, I thought that my mother was the most beautiful woman in the world. She had perfect brown skin and beautiful natural hair. Just like me. Now here's where the hard part comes. Forgiveness.

As I'm writing this part of my story, there are tears rolling down my face because even to this day, it is hard for me to think that my mother didn't love me as a child. I wasn't a difficult child. I was great in school and never got in to trouble. I was afraid to. I was afraid that my mother would hate me more. You see, I did everything perfect so that my mother wouldn't hate me. I got good grades. I kept my room clean. I came home when the street lights came on. As a matter of fact, I stayed in the house most of the time because I didn't want her to be mad at me. I stayed out of her way. I didn't want her to yell at me. I didn't want her to keep looking at me like I was the worst thing that ever happened to her.

In spite of all that I went through as a child, my mom did some pretty amazing things when I got older. When I was nineteen and a freshman in college, I got pregnant. I thought my mom would hate me for sure, but she didn't. She told me that I was going to finish college on time. When my son was born, my mother took care of him during the day so that I could go to school and work. She wasn't sleep. She helped me. Maybe all those years she slept during the day and I was upset about it, she was storing up her sleep so that she could care for my son during the time when I needed her.

When I graduated from college and got my first job

working for the federal government, she came into my room the night before my first day and told me she was proud of me. She didn't say she loved me, but she said she was proud of me. She wasn't sleep. That was amazing to me!

When I moved out on my own for the first time, it was difficult to make ends meet and take care my son. My mom helped me. My son lived with her until he was 13. I saw him every day and he came home with me on the weekends. She wasn't sleep. She helped me.

Back to that day in the hospital.

My mother was sick and she needed someone to take care of her. She wasn't married, all of her children were grown and she wasn't close with her siblings. She was also germ phobic and had a mild case of obsessive-compulsive disorder or OCD, just like me. As I watched the doctors examining her in the hospital bed, I couldn't help but wonder should I leave her here alone like she left me alone to graduate by myself, experience my menstruation cycle by myself, or figure out life by myself? She didn't comfort me when I was a child. Why should I comfort her? I kept thinking, leave now and don't look back. Sure, she did some things for you when you became an adult, but what about all the stuff that happened when you were a child? A little girl who needed her mother to protect her and tell her that she was beautiful when everyone else was saying otherwise. A little girl who wanted a hug, but was pushed away when she reached out to the one person that could save her. Why should I help her? She doesn't deserve it! She was mean and nasty and a horrible mother! I'm leaving now!!! Wait....I'm trying to turn away. I turned away from her to walk down the corridor and out the door never to look back, but as I turned away, I did look back. I looked back and I saw my mother laying in the bed staring at the wall while the doctors continued to examine her. I saw her face and she looked alone.

Oh my GOD! I know that feeling! Alone! I remember that feeling! It is the worse feeling in the world to be alone with no one to talk to and no one to help you and I don't wish that feeling on anyone! I remember praying right at that moment for GOD to help me and to tell me what to do. I'm angry, I'm upset and I'm confused! GOD, what should I do? I remember reciting one of the Ten Commandments, "Honor thy mother and father." Then I remember, "Forgive." What? FORGIVE?

Okay, so forgive my mother? YES! Forgive her for everything bad that she has ever done to me? YES! Why? Because you cannot be the daughter that you need to be right now for your mother unless you forgive her. I remember thinking, really GOD? You see, I talk to my Heavenly Father every day. I have conversations with Him like He is right in front of me and He is. He is with me always and He was with me when I forgave my mother. As I stared at her, I began saying to myself, 'Ma, I forgive you. I forgive you for not being the mother that you should have been when I was growing up. I forgive you for not holding me, for not loving me, for not protecting me from you. I forgive you for blaming me because my father wasn't there. You said that he said that children were the "garbage of lovemaking" and for a long time I thought I was garbage. I forgive you both for that one. I forgive you for not telling me that when I turned twelve that I would bleed once a month and it would be okay because it was part of life. I forgive you for calling me ugly because I realize that you have been through some tough times in your life and it's not your fault. I forgive you for not saying you love me. I forgive you for not taking care of me. I forgive you.

Wow, that was tough and I did it. I forgave my mother and now I forgive myself for even thinking about mistreating her in her time of need.

My mother got sick in 2002 and for the next three years her health deteriorated. First, she couldn't walk and then she lost her sight in one eye. She couldn't go to the bathroom without assistance or bathe herself. She couldn't even feed herself. She kept getting fluid on her left lung and then the cancer diagnosis came and then she couldn't do anything and I had to do everything.

That's right, I did everything. I cooked for her. I cleaned for her. I bathed her. I changed her diapers. I fed her. I told her I loved her repeatedly even when she was angry. I told her I loved her when she was sad. I told her I loved her every evening when I left the nursing home and I told her I love her every morning when I went back to the nursing home. I told her not to worry anymore, I'm here and I'm not going to leave you or abandon you. You are not alone.

On April 15, 2005, the doctors told me that the fluid in her lung was not going away and there was nothing more they could do for her. The chemotherapy didn't work and she was getting weaker every day. The only thing that I could do was make her comfortable. They weren't expecting her to make it to the summer. On Mother's Day, I brought balloons to her room and sat with her and watched her sleep. She did that a lot. It's strange because when I was young I was really upset that my mother was always sleeping, but this time, I was actually glad to see her sleeping. It was nice to see her not in pain or having that worried look on her face.

On June 1, 2005, the doctors advised that my mother should be moved to hospice. I signed the papers and they moved her to a nice quiet room. She was sleeping for a while, but she woke up briefly and stared at me. She smiled and closed her eyes and went back to sleep.

On June 2, 2005, my mother turned eighty years old. I brought balloons to her room and sat with her all day. We watched her favorite show, NCIS. Well, I watched it; she slept. They gave her morphine for any pain.

On June 3, 2005, I went to see my mother and she was still sleeping. They took the tube out of her lung because the fluid was filling up faster than they could drain it so they stopped. She looked different. She looked like she was at peace, sleeping quietly. I was at peace as well. I stayed with her until nine that evening and then I went home. I believe at this point, her spirit had left her body. I believe that your spirit leaves your body long before your body shuts down. I believe her spirit was no longer of the body.

On June 5, 2005, around 3:15 p.m., my mother's body stopped functioning. I wasn't there. I received a phone call. You see, the one thing that I was not going to do was watch my mother take her last breath. She asked to be cremated so I figured that my last memories would be of her sleeping peacefully. I was wrong. In order to cremate her, I needed to identify her body! I asked can't you just take my word for it that it's her? No, I was told. I had to identify the body. Now what am I going to do? I don't want to see my mother's lifeless body! I want to remember her sleeping! I called three of my closest friends. When they read this, they will know who they are. They went with me to the funeral home and waited for me while I went into a dimly lit room to see my mother one more time.

There she was, laying on a table, fully covered except for her face. She had the most beautiful face with no wrinkles. The lady couldn't believe that she was eighty. She closed the door to give me some privacy.

I walked over to her and I kissed her forehead. It was cold and she looked like she was sleeping. I then said, "Ma, I know this is not you. This is just your earthly body and how God wants me to remember you on earth. I know that your spirit is free now." I kissed her forehead again and I walked away. This time I didn't look back because I knew she was okay which meant that I was okay. We are both free.

Forgiveness.

I had to forgive my mother so that I could be the daughter that she needed me to be in her time of need.

I say to you, whatever it is, let it go! You cannot function as GOD has planned if you don't. Believe me, you will be a better person and your conscience will be clear.

~INSPIRATION~

I Am Still Standing!
By Sandra L. Fletcher

Have you ever broken up with a boyfriend? How about a divorce? What about a relationship with a close friend that ended? Were you ever fired or down-sized in a job? Has a friend or a loved one died? Has there been a disaster in your life? Anytime there is a sorrowful separation in a relationship, there is a grieving process.

My story begins August 12, 2007. That is a Sunday I will always remember. My church had a prayer basket where members would write down a prayer request and put it in the basket. When entering church a member would pull a slip of paper from the prayer basket and begin praying for the request. Prior to that Sunday I had written my son's name on one slip of paper and my husband's name on another slip of paper. This particular Sunday the presence of God was in the "house" and I had an unusual praise and worship for God. After service there was so much joy in me. My daughter, grandson, and friend of my daughter's went to Outback to eat. I came home still filled with joy. The phone rang. One of my son's friends called and was crying and kept repeating my son's name, Johnnie. Finally he said, "He's gone, he's gone." While riding his motorcycle, my son had been hit by an SUV and instantly died. He was only 36 years old and engaged to be married. Unknown to me at that time, our mighty prayer warrior, the church Chief Intercessor, had pulled my son and husband's name and had prayed for both of them that morning. Before I knew about my son's death, God had already sent the Holy Spirit to comfort me. Learning that both my husband and son were prayed for hours before my son's death comforted me.

My son's death was the beginning of many deaths of family members and close friends. My husband's step mother died 3 days after our son. She lived out of state and we didn't know that she died until months later. Then in September 2007, the matriarch of my mother's family died. We had a close relationship. In October 2007, my husband's brother died followed by a sister in March 2008. In the same month of March one of our best friends died. Another family friend died in June. My oldest brother died July 20, 2008, which was on a Sunday. All of these deaths occurred at the same time I was grieving the death of my son.

After 2008 there were, of course, other deaths, but there were two devastating ones. In 2010, my best friend of 51 years died. Our friendship began in 6th grade. I was not prepared for that. I always envisioned us growing old together and sitting in our rocking chairs talking and laughing about our youthful escapades. Then in 2013, my husband of 45 years died. Talk about being shocked. I expected to go first. He would say he was going to live to be 120 years old and I would say I wouldn't be around that long. I had no desire to live that long. After retirement, we truly became one. I never thought there would be a time he would not be in my life or that we would not be together.

I have learned that any broken relationship, not just death, causes grief. There are different causes of grief, but the grieving process is the same. The grieving process is an individual process. There is no right way or wrong way to grieve. I understand that the grieving process is a lonely one. You feel alone going through the process. No one can grieve for you; but, you are not really alone. You have God, family and friends to support you through the process. When our son was killed, my husband and I had each other as well as a support system. We had each other through the many deaths since 2007. When my husband died, I missed having his physical support. This was a tough one for me. I thought the death of a child was tough, but no longer having my spouse was tougher.

In the midst of grieving, you don't think you will get through it. Sometimes it seems to be more than what you can handle. You don't see a light at the end of the tunnel. But, let me tell you how I made it through the storm and why I am still standing. It's my faith. I am a Christian and I can only tell you what I know. God is my anchor. He is the rope I have been clinging to. He sends me comfort through family and friends. Even now, with unbearable days or moments, He has someone from my circle of comfort to reach out to me. It can be a text, phone call or card. Music has been a stabilizer for me. Words from hymns, Bible passages and daily readings are also a part of my support system.

One of the bible scripture helping me cope is, "Trust in the Lord with all thine heart; and lean not unto thine own understanding. In all thy ways acknowledge Him, and He shall direct thy paths." Proverbs 3:5-6 (KJV)

Prayer is a tremendous help. My prayers and most definitely prayers of others help with the grieving process. Some days when the grief was unbearable and I could not pray, I could feel the prayers and love of others. Reading about grief has let me know that I am not the only one grieving. Just talking with someone also grieving helps both of us. When asked, don't hesitate to be truthful. If you are having a bad moment, say it. Just remember grieving is a process and there is no time frame for grieving. Try not to be alone when you are having a bad day. Call someone, leave the house, and help someone. God chose me to experience broken relationships through death. Some people say I am a strong woman. I say it is the God in me that gives me the strength to endure.

~Flawless~

We're In This Thing Together
By Teresa Graves

Just Believe
God answers prayers and makes dreams come true. He's amazing and waiting for you. Whether you are looking for love, direction, purpose, healing or peace, I pray that God soon delivers your needs and desires. Hold on, He has not forgotten you.

The Challenge
Look in the mirror and cover your ears from the world. Don't allow others to tell you who you are. Your name is not in the dictionary, so only you can define you. You were chosen to be you and starting now, I challenge you to be the best you, you can be.

Did You Know?
Did you know you are never alone? You are loved, valued and you matter!

Never Too late
It's never too late to start over again; no one is perfect. Don't be afraid to seek your joy. Take forward the lessons you've learned by now and allow your mind and patience to determine your next choice. Leave the bitterness behind along with the walls you want to put up. Without walls, it will be easier to hug you, lift you up, and cheer you on!

Get Up
As you go through life, know that your past will not affect your future. You failed at some things, but you are not a

failure. You have lost some things, but you are not a loser. What you have been through hasn't broken you, but will make you stronger, wiser and a winner.

Love

I love the person I have become. I fought long and hard to become her. I have to love me inside and out before I can embrace another. I am wonderfully made and God handpicked me for this journey. I will survive, I will be whole, I will succeed and I will make a difference with my presence. I am loving the skin I'm in and I am at a place where I will bury the hurt, disappointment and anger of yesterday. Today, I will live like the queen I am. My dash will matter and so will yours.

~Encouragement~

No Matter What
By Kimberly P. Carter

Good times or bad times
Happiness or sadness
Friends or Foe
Sickness or health
Employed or unemployed
Unpaid bills or paid bills
Laughter or pain
Light or darkness
Commitment or non-commitment
Sunshine or rain
Loyalty or betrayal

Remember, *No Matter What* is going on in our lives, we must trust and believe that God is in control! We are equipped for such times as these.

No Matter What the situation is, we must Stay Rooted!

"Be cheerful *No Matter What*; pray all the time; thank God *No Matter What* happens. This is the way God wants you, who belong to Christ Jesus, to live."
1 Thessalonians 5:16-18. (The Message)

~UPLIFT~

Inextinguishable Lights
By Barbara Barton

God wants you to be a shining example of Him for He is the Light of the World and the light should be reflected in everything you say and do. God has chosen you to carry the glow of His light as you strive to be the Christian young ladies God has designed for you to be.

Shining your light before others means that you are committed to be a role model for other young ladies who are watching you. You must always strive to do your best and be the best.

Respect others and demand the same in return. You must learn to set the bar high, don't be lazy with just getting by and reach for the top. Let nothing stop you from reaching your goals; who knows where the future can lead you if you aim high and just imagine if you have faith as small as a mustard seed, you can say to any mountain, "Move from here to there" and it will move. Nothing will be impossible for you because nothing is too hard for God.

Image is everything and you should be aware of who you are at all times, even when you think no one is watching. Learn to push beyond the odds, stay focused and pray that God will use you to be a blessing.

Say connected to God by learning more of His Word at every opportunity that is presented to you. Be it the preached Word, Sunday School or other teachings, you must hear the Word, apply the Word and then walk in the Word of God.

Use your inextinguishable light and never let it burn out

because you are our future. God has given you parents and mentors who He has chosen and equipped to help lead and guide you into that future that has a light that never burns out, that never dims and is full of possibilities. These parents and mentors sacrifice their time, energy and talents to help you grow in Him and achieve your goals. Use them as a beacon as you make your way through life, trying to discover who you are and what you want to be. They will help you see that the sky is the limit!

This is just the beginning for you so keep pushing forward, no turning back, never ever quit, continue to let your light shine for others to follow and always remember who you are. You are a beautiful flower and no matter the obstacles in life, your have within you an inextinguishable light that will burn bright as long as you stay the path.

~AWARENESS~

Who Are They – A Short Story
By Cheryl Barton

"Tracee, are you ready to go?"

Kortney looked at her best friend with a face full of frustration at the length of time it was taking her to get dressed.

"Kortney I'm going as fast as I can. You know I have to have the perfect look. I can't go out looking any kind of way."

"We're only going to the mall to shop for school clothes. What's the big deal?"

Kortney didn't understand the change in her best friend. They have been best friends since elementary school and now they were both entering high school together and excited about the upcoming first day of school. The biggest excitement around a new school year was going shopping for school clothes. They were happy that they were attending a school that didn't have a specific dress code which also meant they both needed to be dressed in the latest gear if they wanted to be noticed. At least that's what Tracee told her. She had different ideas on learning to be just who she was without trying to impress other people.

Kortney watched as her best friend threw one outfit after the other across the bed.

"The big deal is that we may run into some of the kids from the school and then on the first day they could recognize me from being dressed down and I'll live with that stigma forever."

"Tracee, you are way too concerned about what everyone else thinks, especially about what you have on. Don't you know there are kids our age who have one outfit to wear every day and are happy they have that? You have two closets full of stuff and your biggest concern is if someone else likes what they see you in."

"Stop acting like the way you dress doesn't matter to you Kortney. You know what they say! You're only a part of the in-crowd when you wear what everyone else is wearing as far as the top fashion for the season."

"Really Tracee? Who are they?"

Tracee stopped going through her clothes and turned toward Kortney.

"Why are you acting all crazy Kortney? Why are you getting an attitude about clothes?"

"I'm not getting an attitude. I'm simply asking you who they are."

"What?" Tracee said looking perplexed.

"Every time you talk about fashion or make-up you always say 'they say' and I want to know who they are."

"Girl you know. They are the people who write fashion columns and they are those people who tell you what is and is not hot. They set the tone and the standard for fashion and style and if you don't follow them then you're nobody."

"So I'm a nobody if I don't let someone I don't know, someone who doesn't define who I am and someone who doesn't pay for anything that I have, tell me how to dress? So you live your life according to these 'they' people?"

"Kortney stop making this into something bigger than it

is. All I'm saying is I take pride in how I look and that way I won't end up being the person having fingers pointed at me and being snickered at and I'll always be a part of the "it" crowd because I'm always fly! Girl, we are nothing if we are not trending when it comes to fashion and style. Without that we are just nothing."

Kortney decided to let the conversation go because clearly they were not on the same page when it came to how important what they looked like to others was. She felt it was time Tracee got a lesson in how clothes don't make the person and she had the perfect way to prove it to her.

"Hey Tracee, before we go to the mall I need to make a quick stop at the library first."

"Okay, sure. Let's go."

Tracee followed Kortney into the library and up to the second level where a young woman sat alone in a quiet corner studying. She watched as Kortney walked right up to her.

"Hey Carmen!" Kortney said.

"Hey Kortney. What are you doing here? I was expecting your brother. Did he send you to tell me he wasn't coming?"

"No. He told me you would be here and I wanted to stop in and say hi while you were in town. This is my friend Tracee."

Tracee looked at Kortney's friend and wondered who she was. She gave Carmen a once over and noticed her clothes were from at least ten years ago. Her tennis were no names and so were her jeans. Her top was a plain white shirt and her face had no make-up besides a little lip gloss. Even though she was clearly very pretty lots of make-up was the trend these days and clearly this girl didn't have it. Though her hair was neat it didn't have a lot of style to it and her nails didn't even have any polish on them. Who was this plain Jane, Tracee thought?

"Tracee, this is Carmen a friend of my brother's."

She knew it would be rude to not speak so she uttered a light hello.

"Hello Carmen."

"Hi Tracee," Carmen said. "Nice to meet you. You look very nice. Where are you girls heading out to a party or something?"

"No, we're just going to the mall."

"Are you coming along with us Carmen? I'm sure you could probably pick up a few nice things?" Tracee said with judgment in her voice.

Kortney was glad Carmen didn't pick up on how snide Tracee was trying to be, but she knew Tracee's lesson would soon come.

"No I have some studying to do."

"On a Friday? Who studies on a Friday?"

"I do if I plan to make something of myself one day. Education is important. How are your grades?" Carmen asked Tracee.

Kortney stood back and watched the scene play out.

"Oh my grades are okay. Of course, I'm planning to be in the fashion industry, so I'm not all that worried about school. I have to be sure I look the part more than I need to act the part, if you know what I mean."

"Not really, but humor me. I see you are laced in the finest fashion right now, especially for a trip to the mall, but I'm not hating. You look very nice, but you'll need to do more than just look nice even in the fashion world."

"Well some people do books and I do looks and I'm not hating either, if you catch my drift."

Kortney smiled at all the shade that was being thrown, but she didn't intervene. She knew Carmen had this.

"Oh, yes I catch it with no problem. I admire your style, but style isn't everything and it shouldn't make you who you are or who you plan to be. Isn't there more to you than just what you have on?"

"In this day and age, what you look like is everything. You have to have the long, tight weave like mine, the coke-bottle figure, a behind that you can rest a quarter on and it won't fall off and your gear has to be top of the line. What good is all that education if no one wants to be friends with you or even be around you because you don't fit the mold of what society says you should look like?"

Kortney then chimed in.

"Carmen, my friend Tracee here has the "they" mentality where it doesn't matter what she thinks of herself, it only matters what others think of her, especially of what she has on. In her mind she is nothing if she isn't turning heads when she walks into a room."

"Is that so?" Carmen asked.

Tracee turned to Kortney with a look that said she wasn't happy with being put on the spot.

"Kortney is exaggerating, but yes I like to stay with the

latest fashions and I think it's a big part of who you are and who you'll become."

"So you're saying I'm not somebody important if I don't have labels on everything I wear?"

"I'm not saying that about you, I'm only talking about me here."

"So, you didn't take a good, long look at me when you came in and judged me?" Carmen asked.

Tracee said nothing. She wondered how this outing to the library turned around to be about her.

"I'm just saying that you're sitting here in a library on a Friday afternoon studying by yourself and I don't see any friends around. Clearly you didn't really care much about who saw you because you have on the plainest clothes I've ever seen on a female. Not judging, but you look like you didn't really care what you put on when you left your house. I'm not throwing shade or anything; I'm just saying you can catch more bees with honey."

"Who says I'm trying to catch anything?"

Tracee started to feel bad. She didn't know how the conversation had taken such a terrible turn.

"I'm sorry Carmen. I'm really not judging you. I'm just explaining me."

"Tracee, I know you don't mean any harm and if you're paying attention, I'm not upset at all. I'm actually enjoying this conversation with you. I come across young ladies all the time who think just as you do. I don't consider them all as judgmental, though some are, but I don't think every book should be judged by its cover. I think the important parts are what's in between the pages of the book. I respect that you love to be beautiful and fly at all times. There is nothing wrong with that, but make sure you don't think that's all you are. Don't live by the standards someone set in a magazine, but be the standard by recognizing who you are, with or without the hottest fashions. I could drip myself in the greatest fashions, but I'm more concerned about why would I want to base who I am on what I see in a magazine or read in a column. Just make sure, again, that's not all you see in yourself because you are more than that."

"Tracee is good people Carmen. She just doesn't think far beyond her closet."

"Sure I do Kortney. There you go exaggerating again."

"Really Tracee? We are going to the mall and you have on four inch heels. Who does that and why?"

"These are the latest Manolo's girl! I wouldn't be seen in anything but the best."

"Is that your best Tracee? Your outward appearance? What about what's inside?"

"They don't see or care about what's inside. It's all about what they see when they first look at you."

"Who are they?" Carmen asked.

Kortney looked at Tracee and smiled.

"I asked her the same question. She has these mysterious 'they' people who are the authors and finishers of her life. She bases what she wears everyday on this mysterious group of people."

Tracee looked embarrassed. Why was she being harassed simply because she liked to look nice?

"What is this, pick on Tracee day?"

"Not at all Tracee. I think Kortney brought you by here to meet me for a reason."

"Why would she do that?"

"I think it's to prove to you that there is more to someone than meets the eye."

"Okay, game over. Somebody tell me what's going on here," Tracee exclaimed.

"First, tell me what was your first thought when you saw me," Carmen asked.

"Okay, I'll play along. I always look a person over when I meet them, so I saw that your gear is all plain, nothing special. I don't see any make-up and though your hair is nice, you could really hook it up if you added a weave and a nice cut to it."

"I would do that why? If you haven't noticed, my hair is long and full already. Why would I weave it up?" Carmen asked.

"I know. I'm just saying weaves are the thing these days. You never know who you could meet. You could meet the man of your dreams and he could be rich and famous and sweep you off of your feet and take you away where you'd never have to worry about studying again because he'd take care of you. He wouldn't notice you dressed like that. There are fashion magazines for a reason and they all say you are what you look like."

"There's that mysterious 'they' again," Kortney said.

"Stop it Kortney. It's what all the latest fashion magazines say, so it must be true."

"Tracee, there is nothing wrong with fashion as long as you know that's not the most important thing in life. At your age, make sure you focus on your education as well and don't worry so much about what others think about how you look. When you don't meet their high standards, you'll fall so fast you won't know how to pick yourself back up because you were so dependent upon what someone else thought of how you looked. I could tell when you first walked up to me that the first thing you did was judge me by what I had on. I'm not mad about it."

"So now who are you and why did Kortney bring me here to meet you."

"My name is Carmen, yes, but it's not the name you would recognize. My middle name is Carmen. My first name is Arianna."

Nothing rang a bell to Tracee so she looked to Kortney for help.

"Tracee, what's the name of the biggest fashion magazine around?"

"That's easy, it's On Top Magazine". That's the number one fashion magazine in the world. Why?"

Kortney and Carmen both smiled while Tracee continued to look bewildered.

"Tracee, her name is Arianna Mazé. Her father owns On Top Magazine and the fashion line to most of the clothes in your closet!"

"What!!!!!"

Tracee stared at Carmen, bewildered.

"Lies! I don't believe it! Stop playing around with me

Kortney. What would his daughter Arianna be doing sitting here in the library dressed like this studying?"

"Carmen, show her," Kortney said.

Carmen reached in her bag, pulled out one of the On Top magazines and sure enough, inside staring back at her was a very glammed up picture of Carmen with the caption that read, 'Orin Mazé and his daughter, Arianna at fashion week.' There was no way to mistake that the girl in the picture was in fact Carmen.

"Oh my goodness. It is you. I don't understand. Why are you here, in a library studying and how do you know Kortney."

Kortney smiled like the cat had her tongue.

"Kortney you've been holding out on me. What gives?"

"Let me answer first," Carmen said. "I love fashion and I, of course love my dad and my family and I could have anything in the world I want, but what I want most is my law degree. I grew up wearing everything that was top of the line, but it didn't make me happy as some people may think it would. I wanted to be more than just pictures on and in magazines. It took me a few years to get away from the person you see in that picture and to become the person you see sitting here much happier. My family is part of the 'they' that you keep referring to and believe me, we don't even believe the stuff we write about. It's done to sell fashion and to sell magazines. This, what you see in this magazine, is all for show. I could be glammed up and walk around in the finest, but I choose not to because for once in my life, I want to be taken seriously for who I am in between the pages and not just the cover."

Tracee now understood. She was spending all of her time focusing on what she looked like and not really on who she was. Clothes didn't really tell you anything about a person because clearly she misread who Carmen was.

"I'm sorry for judging you by your clothes."

"It's okay Tracee. Just make sure you care just as much about the inside as you do about the outside."

"Okay, one question has been answered, but I have another. How do you know Kortney?"

Kortney chimed in the answer.

"She's dating my brother. They met in law school and have been dating for about a year. She's in town for a few days to visit him while they both prepare to take the bar exam. My brother swore us all to secrecy. They're engaged to be married now so I asked Carmen if it was okay if I introduced you and she agreed. I just wanted you to see that the outside doesn't tell you a lot about who a person is. You have always been so hooked on who you are on the outside that I wanted to you finally see you can be and are much more than that. You know how plain my brother is and look who he snagged!"

"She's right Tracee. You are much, much more and believe me the 'they' do what they do to make money, not necessarily because it's the gospel. Take it for what it is, but don't make it who you are. The 'they don't know you, but in order for them to stay relevant, they have to have a way to continually draw you in. Be you and get that education. Let your Mr. Right get to know who you are and not just what you look like. I looked just like this when her brother and I met and we fell in love with who we are on the inside. It took him months to find out who I was and that was because I told him. At that point I had to because we wanted the families to meet."

"Well this has been enlightening. Never judge a book by its cover couldn't be any truer than it is right now."

"That's good to know. Well I don't want to keep you ladies from the mall. Have fun shopping and Kortney, bring her by the hotel tomorrow before I leave and we can all do lunch."

"I will," Kortney replied.

Tracee smiled, relieved at how the conversation turned into a lesson learned for her.

"First, though, we're going back to my house so that I can put on some shoes that I can comfortably shop in," Tracee added before following Kortney out.

As they left the library, Tracee turned to Kortney.

"I've been acting a little crazy about outer appearance lately haven't I?"

"Yeah you have and you made more than a few mentions of 'they' like it was all you depended on for who you are and I knew differently."

"Well, no more 'they' for me. Who are they anyway? I'm more about me and what's in between the pages and not just my cover."

~INCREASE~

Emmanuel Come Down
By Michelle Russell

Emmanuel come down from you high heavenly place
Emmanuel come down and be loved face to face
Emmanuel come gentle Keisha's mother is crying
Emmanuel come powerful Myriah's brothers are dying

Emmanuel come loving Jody's heart is breaking
Emmanuel come peaceful Lata's country is blazing
Emmanuel come merciful Lena's sins are abounding
Emmanuel come tender Jackie's hurt is compounding

Emmanuel come faithful Rachel's trust is diminished
Emmanuel come restore Tina's sister thinks it's finished
Emmanuel come now Tianna's resolve is breaking
Emmanuel come saving Jessie's soul is for the taking

Emmanuel come please Phyllis' tears are her friends
Emmanuel come healing Mama Keeps announcing her end
Emmanuel come with salvation my sisters need freeing
Emmanuel come with haste we need you for our being

~GREATER~

No Regrets – Unselfish Acts of Awesomeness
By LaTonya Summerville

You shouldn't do that, it's not a good idea, historically it has never worked, and there will not be a positive outcome - I'm telling you, take my experience as an example, save yourself the frustration, hurt and trouble and don't do it!

Has anyone ever told you this? What did you do? If you went on and followed through with what you were being talked out of, are you sorry you did so? If you didn't follow through with it, are you satisfied with your decision?

Imagine a world full of hate and a world that fully accepts demoralizing others simply because of the color of their skin. Next imagine you hearing the call from God to be the one to change things in a movement that is peaceful, diplomatic and non-violent. In case you don't know who I'm referring to, keep reading. If you do know who I'm referring to, keep reading.

Total action is required of a passionate person with a calling and sense of urgency to intercede inhumanity. Every one of us is born with a purpose to fulfill and a passion for something. If a person never acts on their purpose their soul will feel forever empty.

My husband and I both made a decision to try and alleviate some mayhem because we had the opportunity and resources to do so. We went against the popular decision and came out bruised and victimized, but with much more wisdom than we previously had. Do we regret it? No we don't. Would we do it again? Yes we would because one of our beliefs is that everyone deserves a chance. Did we learn a lesson? Yes, we learned several lessons and we would make adjustments in our quest to help, but we would definitely do it again.

There was a man who answered the call to change the way the United States of America and even the world treated and viewed people of color. He was born on January 15, 1929 and he had the "American Dream". He had an education, wife, home, children and a decent job. Instead of him being content and enjoying what so many others wanted, he reached deep down in his heart and reached back to hold the door for those that were coming behind him, near and afar. We all have benefited from his unselfish acts.

Thank you Dr. Martin Luther King, Jr. I am forever grateful for you. As a people we will strive every day to do better. Incidentally or as destiny would have it, our President Barack Obama, a man of color was sworn in for his second term as the leader of the United States of America. This happened the same day that we celebrated Dr. King's (January 21, 2013).

Whether you are Independent, Republican or Democrat, who can deny the awesomeness of that. I promise you we won't and should not minimize this milestone.

~Trust~

Party of One
By Jaye Matthews

Today, as I sit in Starbucks reflecting back over my life, there have been some victories and accomplishments that I am proud of and there have been some regrets.

I think my reflection comes from waking up, and realizing that in less than two months, I'll be forty years old. I'm baffled and shocked. I mean, I know my age, but it seems like high school was just yesterday and time has flown by so very quickly. I feel like I went to bed at eighteen and woke up at thirty-nine and holding. What have I done with the time? I was determined to accomplish my goals, both scholastically and professionally, to travel and go as I please, to save and spend what I want, to date here and there and perhaps love as long as it lasted.

I've had an amazing, independent, free-spirited single life. However, I can't ignore the fact that while living this great life, I have panicked because I have always desired true love, marriage and children, and it just never really seemed to be within my grasp or even within my view. People assume that it's something that we single, professional, independent women don't want just because we don't have it. I say we just live it up and make the best out of our single status until God sends the man He created us specifically for and allows him to find us; in His time, of course.

I recall my first struggle with my single status. I was thirty-five and so frustrated. I was frustrated with love and relationships, with myself, and also with God's process, if I can be honest and transparent for a second. My friends were married with children and some of closest friends may not have been married, but had children and grandchildren. Yet, here I was, over thirty-five and considered "high risk" even if I ever did end up having children. I always wanted five boys; however, the older I got the less my number got. At this time, I was down to just hoping for one. I felt like something was wrong with me.

My relationships had been good and some great; however, they didn't work out for countless reasons. For example, one of my best loves had trust and commitment issues. As a result, that was on and off for about ten years. Finally, when I met another, who was amazing and wanted all in, he was in Florida and wanted me to move, instantly, from Maryland which to me was unrealistic at the time. I was tired; tired of my relationships not working out, tired of being alone and feeling lonely, tired of standing in belief that God would move on my behalf regarding this matter and actually allow me to be found and super tired of working hard to remain celibate. I was tired of not having an actual shoulder to cry on beyond God's, my parents' and my sister-friends' and I was tired of doing everything with my girlfriends. I wanted and longed for safety and security in the arms and life of a true man of God who loved and adored me in an uninhibited way and for all the right reasons.

I remember coming in one night after church and tucking in with God. I prayed and cried out like never before and I actually prayed myself to sleep. I like to call it being "spooned by Jesus." My prayer was for God to show up on my behalf as it relates to who He has created me for, by way of a man, and to allow him to find me.

All the things that I previously shared here with you are what I openly and honestly told God. I told Him what I was tired of, what I longed for and I also told Him that I didn't want to disappoint Him by falling sexually, but my celibacy ties were wearing rather thin. I made sure to thank Him for keeping me, for being my protector and provider and for blessing me to be able to do it all by myself throughout my adult lifetime. However, I told God just because I can do it all by myself, doesn't mean I want to continue to do it all alone. I wanted to be found by my soul mate, the one who would make me his wife. I knew that I didn't want just any man just to say I had I man because that was never the issue. I wanted the right one for me and I wanted it to be my last, first everything. I'm talking about date, kiss, engagement, marriage, everything.

I started to compromise in my prayer because I thought perhaps I'm being unrealistic, but then I remembered the God I serve. I wanted him to be saved, unmarried, no children, educated, gainfully employed, financially sound, handsome, fun, a visionary, ambitious, my ultimate best friend! I know, I asked for too much, right?

Well, I prayed that prayer, on a Friday night, and he found me the very next day. A handsome, single, never been married, no kids having, saved, ambitious, fun-loving, caring, protective, financially secure man of vision. God did just that and to top it all off, he's a Pastor. After connecting I learned that he's longed for the same and was told in prophecy that he would meet his wife in a certain way and at a certain place (I don't' want to disclose that). Guess what? That's how we met. In addition, we realized that we had crossed paths twice before and each time he remembered me by my smile. So many things that took place, that are evidence that God set us up and if I tried to share them all, I would be writing forever. Our connection is definitely a blessing and our story is a true God Story. While I know that now, I want to be totally honest with you, my sisters; I almost rejected my blessing and I want to share about that because I want you to be mindful and learn from my mistake.

Even though I prayed deliberately and intentionally for him to find me, I guess I didn't know that God would do it so instantaneously, literally the next day! I now know what people mean when they say, "Be careful what you pray for." I asked God to do it, and to move quickly on my behalf and He did just that. I loved this instant catapult into love at first sight and instantly committed to my gift that God sent to find me per his request; however, it was such a culture shock for someone like me who, as an only child, was raised by a single mom, had been mostly in on-off relationships, single, and living alone all of my adult life from age eighteen to almost forty. I wasn't used to frequent calls just to say hello or ask what I dream about or desire, texts to see if I made it safely from A to B, emails during the work day just to say I'm thinking about you or someone telling me that his main goal in life moving forward is to insure my happiness and to keep a smile on my face every single day. This was all new.

To be honest, I became overwhelmed after two weeks of

receiving love that was pure, consistent, and real. Why? I didn't know what that looked like. I didn't recognize it because I never had it from a man, romantically in this way. Therefore, I rejected it, or at least attempted to. Still, it amazes me that I really understand, through this, that what God has for us is indeed for us. This man, refused to give up on me and on being with me even though I threw in the towel saying that I didn't want it anymore because it was "too much" and I became fearful of that which I never recognized and couldn't identify, which is called the unfamiliar, True Love. He gave me my space, but still believed that I was created for him and that I was the one that he still chose to be his future wife. He would send me messages consistently during this period of time saying things like, "Even when you have not-so-good days, I will still love you and want you." How amazing is that? That's true unconditional love. That's what really hit me, that this man loves me, with the love of The Lord.

After disregarding calls, texts, Google+ posts, and Instagram pleas for about two weeks I finally decided to respond to one of the emails that he sent me, which simply said, "I miss you" because truth be told I really missed him too. I thought about him, prayed for him, dreamt about him and I knew I loved him, but I was fighting it. Still, he made himself completely vulnerable to me, allowing his truth to be known even after I retreated for a couple of weeks ceasing all communication thinking it was over simply because I was overwhelmed by real love. Never did he judge me, blame me or point a finger at me. He was elated to hear back from me and wanted to pick up loving me where he never actually left off.

Today, we're exclusively courting. How cute is that? We're genuine friends who love each other and with each day that passes it becomes more comfortable for both of us as he's learning to give me time and space to adjust and I'm learning to invite him in more closely and intimately. We support one another, talk about our dreams, fears and frustrations and we discuss plans for the future; our future. The man that I always envisioned, the kind of relationship I've always longed for, the ring and wedding dress that I've always dreamed of, they are all within my grasp now because I was bold enough to pray for it and humble myself enough to make it right when I almost messed by blessing up completely.

Sisters, I'd like to encourage you to pray deliberately and diligently for what it is that you want in a husband, but I urge you to be ready when God delivers because He will do it when you're least expecting it. Ultimately, God knows when you're ready because He's the one who is preparing you for your King. I know that we lose hope in the process, but understand that God is working in your waiting and that He has not forgotten about you. While you're waiting, literally WAIT. I've been celibate for nearly five years. It hasn't been easy, but doing it my way wasn't working and left me single, empty, guilty and disgusted. That's why I decided to try doing it God's way. Celibacy isn't easy, namely when you know how amazing sex is and can be (and I know). I will be the first to stand up and say that it is very difficult, but with much prayer, fasting and exercise (smile), I have endured.

Lastly, when he comes, be ready to fully receive him. Men tend to think that we single, professional, independent women don't really need them and men want and need to be needed. Allow yourselves to receive what comes with him which should be him opening doors and car doors, calls to see if you arrived at work safely, offering to help you with a bill or two and paying the entire dinner bill and not just his half, just to name a few.

God created men to be our covering so allow him to operate in his role and cover you. I learned that there are men in our generation who are still real men no matter what society says about them and no matter how the media tries to portray them and it doesn't matter how stubborn our independence tries to resist them. We've been doing it solo for our adult lifetimes and for me I am happy to say that God has sent me help and has well prepared me to be a help to him in life and in ministry as well. All I know as a preacher's kid (PK) myself is that I'm excited about potentially wearing the new hat of "First Lady," in the future, but I don't want to literally wear the hats since I can't mess my hair up, I have plans to be more than that just a hat.

Sisters I am truly rejoicing because I don't have to check in with hostesses at restaurants anymore as the party of one because he does that for us and now, it's a party of two!

~ENLIGHTEN~

But Still I Stand
by Geezie Reaves

The day it happened I was totally stunned and devastated. I felt the coldness and I just wanted to die inside. No sign, no hint, no idea that such a thing could or would happen to me. I was going through what I thought was enough; with a new job search, family issues and not to mention that I was a single mother running a house whole with two male children. I always thought that if I treated people the way I wanted to be treated, I would have the better things happen in my life. Besides I always prayed!!

The Early Years

It all started in the fall of 1984 when I thought my life had just crashed right before my eyes. I had been married for two short years. During that time I gave birth to two healthy and amazing sons.

My first son, Antonio Dametrius, was born on August 28, 1982 and the second son, Julius Angelo arrived on February 22, 1984. Six months after Julius was born the marriage went south. I was so embarrassed and I felt that everyone would make fun of me due to the circumstances that caused the crumbling of my marriage. I went to my Pastor for counseling, but my heart could not stand the embedded pain. All I could think of over and over was that God did not make a fool, so I made the decision to take my babies (2 years old and 6 months old) and move on. I did not understand clearly at the time, but I did know that if it were not for God in the midst of the situation, I would have been totally lost.

After a short search, my sons and I moved into a new apartment in a different area of town. Life with my sons was good mainly because we had each other and I kept God in the midst. I prayed even when I did not understand because I knew that God would not bring me this far to leave me. After living in the apartment for a few years, I found a nice row house where the boys would have more room for growth and play. The new home was still in a pretty good area on the eastside and it was located directly across the street from Baltimore City Truck #15 Fire station.

While living at this location I met a new male companion who, after a few dating years, became my second husband. My new husband (Mr. Firefighter) took the boys to the barbershop every week, helped them with their homework and he even attended monthly meetings at their school. He shared the responsibility of raising my sons in the absence of their estranged father.

We went to church Sunday after Sunday to give God the praises for the blessings in our lives. All went pretty well for at least six years, but the marriage did not work out for more reasons than one. I was back on my knees asking God for new direction and safety for my sons, and God again picked me up and directed my path.

The Second Time Around

It is now 1994, ten years later and here I was again a single mother facing the struggles of raising two sons. Time was moving forward and there was some change in the atmosphere. The boys were arriving in their teen years, I started a new career in Corrections and we found a new place to call home in Baltimore County.

The boys began to meet and mingle with a new variety of mischievous friends. They started doing new and mysterious things and they had their first of many encounters with the law. It was a little rough for the boys, not having a man around, so I enrolled them in a recreation football league and the Rights of Passage organization. This would allow them to do boy stuff and be around potential male role models.

I guess they were not busy enough with school and football because I experienced the shock of my life when I was told that I was going to be a grandmother. My youngest son at fifteen years old was going to be a father. I was in a state of shock and it took me the entire nine months to come to the reality that this was indeed true. Once my Lil princess, Iyanna E. Reaves was born, I found myself transform into a brand new mode. I was very thankful and excited that God blessed me with my first grandchild. She was in great health and as cute as a button. The first few years of her life her Dad, my baby boy, spent time in the juvenile corrections facility. I had a busy schedule with working two jobs to help provide for my granddaughter. I managed to take Iyanna to see her Daddy as often as I could. It is amazing what you can do when you have God in your life. He will definitely give you the strength you need.

The Last Days

The time came when I felt that I was ready to purchase my first home and God had blessed me with the means to do so. I was so excited about this new venture for me and my sons. It only took a few months search and I found a real nice property. I was in deed thankful and I looked forward to getting settled in our new home. Antonio and Julius were even more excited because they each would have their own bedroom and a fully finished basement.

The beginning years in the new house went great. The boys transitioned well and they got along with the other adolescents in the new neighborhood. To keep them busy, we became new members of The YMCA and the boys took their first professional swimming lessons. Even though they had swimming, choir and other activities, they had rare moments when they wanted to show off at school. As they got older their behaviors began to progress in a negative manor in association with the company they kept. When they reached their high school years, trouble settled over my boys. At this point, I was busy trying to find new programs that helped keep my young men on the right path and free from incarceration.

Regardless of how much I tried to keep my sons busy in positive surroundings, they got older and found ways to stay out in the world. Some years past and I ran out of ammunition, but I never gave up because I knew that God would have the last and ultimate solution.

It was a bright spring afternoon on Friday, March 12, 2004. I got off from a tiring day at work, fought through traffic to pick up my granddaughter and I was simply worn out. I had just arrived home and all I saw right away was the flashing light on my answering machine. When I retrieved my messages I had at least six new messages telling me that something had happened to Antonio, my first born. The last and final message said specifically that he had been shot and his body was found on the street. What a horrible way to find out that your child was killed. Frantically I screamed and cried. Once I gained some composure and came out of my coma, the first call I made was to my mother. I screamed "MOM, HE'S GONE"!! At twenty-one years old, Antonio had been shot down on the streets of Baltimore City.

My relationship with God is so much better at this stage in my life. I've learned how to 'Trust in the Lord with all my heart'. I pray daily and worship God with all my heart because I realize that no matter what I go through in life 'I can do all things through Christ that gives me strength'.

I am currently pursuing a new career as a police officer, going to school to pursue my bachelor's degree in Criminal Justice and I am working on my first inspirational publication. God has blessed me with a new grandson and Julius and his wife DeLonya named him Jibril Antonio Dametrius in Antonio's honor. God is the Source and the Strength of my life and 'Still I Stand'.

~IMAGINE~

My Fantasy
By Michelle Russell

In my fantasy, you're not a prince, you're a king,
Ruler and giver of most everything.
Ruthless in spirit, kind in heart,
With the wisdom of lords and a passion for art.

In our fantasy kingdom, I am queen,
To your heirs I am mother.
In your morning glory, your passion takes me,
And I become your fantasy lover.

In our fantasy kingdom, I prepare you for war,
Feeding the hunger of your mighty roar.
In your fantasy battles, I stand strong and tall,
Defending our kingdom with my life, with my all.

For our fantasy kingdom there is no end,
And above all else I'll be your friend.
In that fantasy kingdom, you control time,
Your forever is forever mine.

~DREAM~

Two Worlds, One Girl
By Laniece Oliver

Pageant Queen, Dancer, Model and Deaf? At four years old I began dancing and modeling with my best friend Maya and I found out I was Deaf. Being Deaf in a hearing world is hard, but I've learned a lot of things. One of the first things I've learned is how hard it is to communicate with hearing people. Sometimes it was hard to understand what my dance teacher was saying, but Maya always helped out. At five, I got my first hearing aid and I felt happy that I could hear again and things got a little easier.

In 2010, I started third grade at the Maryland School for the Deaf. I was happy to finally meet so many people who were like me, but I couldn't communicate with them either because I didn't know sign language. Then something great happened to me; I met my new best friend Callie. Callie and I both had a love of reading and asked our third grade teacher, Brandie, to help us start a book club for all the kids at school. Callie helped me learn more sign language and I helped her speak more.

On my tenth birthday the greatest thing ever happened to me. For the first time, I was able to bring my hearing best friend together with my Deaf best friend and that was the first time I realized hearing girls and deaf girls are not that different.

Around that very same time, I started competing in pageants. I lost my first pageant, but I didn't cry because it was the most fun I'd ever had. I continue to compete in pageants and it has shown me that I can make a difference in the world.

Competing in pageants, dancing, modeling, and having two best friends, one Deaf and one hearing, gave me the idea to create an organization called Miss Deaf Dream America. I want to help young deaf and hearing girls realize they can do anything they dream of doing and do what they always wanted to do in their lives. I want to bring my deaf and hearing world together just like I did with my best friends and help them realize that we have some of the same issues.

So, to answer the question of am I a Pageant Queen, a Dancer and a Model? Yes I am a Pageant Queen, because I continued to compete and have won two pageants. Yes, I still love to dance with my church dance ministry. Yes, I'm still a model and I have been chosen to be an international runway model for team USA in the World Championship of the Performing Arts.

Being Deaf is not easy, but it has brought so many opportunities in my life that I never thought could happen to me. I know this is just the beginning for me and I can't wait to see what's next. I won't let anything stop me.

~BOND~

Once There Were Three
By Cheryl Barton

March 2010 Journal Entry - Ok, well it's been a little over a month since that day God decided my brother's time on this side was over and we all just, well had to deal with it. That may sound a little off the wall, but that is exactly what had gone through my mind; God saying this is how it is and well just deal. I know it doesn't sound nice, but sometimes honesty isn't nice. It's just honest.

I have been keeping a journal of my thoughts about my brother's death since February 24, 2014 when he passed away. Tonight I went back to that first day and read it all over and relived in my mind all that has taken place since that day.

I then inserted a few pages before that day in my journal and tried to recall other things in days prior to that and noticed how much my mom and I had been talking about my brother. Nothing in particular, but just conversing about him. Even on that day, after a conversation she'd had with him earlier in the day, we were talking on the phone about him up until five minutes before my dad called me telling me that my brother was gone. For a few days, I spooked myself when I realized how quickly life could change. Talk about in the blink of an eye.

One thing my mom and I talked about was the last time I'd seen my brother. I told her it was strange. I had stopped by his house to drop something off and he sent my nephew out to my car to get it. I was about to pull off and my brother came out of the house saying he just wanted to come out and say hi because he hadn't seen me in a few weeks. We'd talked on the phone, but had not seen each other. We talked for a few more minutes and I remember watching him as he walked away and I mentioned to my daughter that he was moving slower than usual. I didn't dwell on it long. That had been a few days prior to his passing away. Back to the that night..

My daughter and I were in the car on our way to Bible study when I stopped to get gas while talking to my mother. I got off the phone to pump the gas and we were back on the road, we had driven about five minutes down Liberty Road when my cell phone rang again and the caller ID said the call was again from my parent's house. I answered in a light-hearted voice thinking it was my mother again and that she'd forgotten to tell me something. What I got when I said hello would forever change the path my life would take. All I heard was my dad crying saying," he's gone Cheryl; Cotton's gone." I could hear my mom crying and screaming in the background and my only response was an immediate, "I'm on my way."

I was at the corner of Liberty Heights and Rogers Avenue at the light and shaking. I hadn't yet told my daughter what was going on so I pulled over to gather myself. I turned to her and told her what had just happened and I think she was more afraid of my non-reaction than anything else. She sat on the edge of her seat not knowing what I was going to do. Her eyes looked at me wondering if I was going to speed to get to my parents, cry and lose control or scream and curse. I looked at her and saw the fear and just said, "I'm okay" over and over again. She didn't say anything; she just stared at me like she was scared to death. I then reassured her and myself again by repeating over and over, "I'm okay, I'm okay, I'm okay". I took a deep breath and my first thoughts at that moment were not my brother, because he was going to be alright. God had just seen to that. He was resting eternally with God, pain free and worry free. My first thoughts were my parents were at home alone and I was not close enough to embrace them and comfort them. I said a prayer to God to lead and guide me through this and to get me safely to my parents.

Before pulling back into traffic, God spoke and said that it was going to take me some time to get to them safely and that I needed to get someone to them fast so that I would know while I was traveling there, they would be okay because someone would be there with them until I arrived. I called family and friends and all immediately made their way to my parents while I calmed down and focused on getting my daughter and I to them in one piece.

My first reaction has always been hysterics so I was surprised at how calm I was. We grow up with death all around us and it's never easy. Neither was this, but God provided the calm that surpassed all understanding I had over where my hysterics was.

I can remember when my cousin died many years ago, I was at work and scared my co-workers I screamed so loud. Back in 2003, my mom called me at work because something had happened to my grandmother. She wouldn't say what because I know she didn't want to upset me. She just told me to come home. I immediately called my brother Cotton who then told me what happened. Of course, the people in my office, again, were subjected to my sudden emotional outburst. In that situation as with so many, my first call had been to my brother Cotton. He was the oldest and always the rock when it came to my two brothers and I. I then realized I wouldn't be able to pick up the phone and lean on him anymore. My brothers have always been my rock and now we were two. Yes, at one time, we were three.

I look back on so many things now and I can remember him being my first phone call in so many situations. My thoughts today are though I didn't talk every day to my brother in person or on the phone, I liked having the option to do so if I needed or just wanted to. That for me is more disturbing than anything. I can't just pick up the phone and talk to him no matter how much I want to. There were days in the past when I probably should have and didn't, but at least the choice to do so was at my fingertips.

My conversations are now one sided. As I stated when I spoke at his funeral, my brothers and I had our roles and his was definitely that rock. My other brother and I are much more emotional and he was always the calm one. He was the one who would listen and the one we would listen to. I think at the moment of his passing, I inherited some of his cool and calmness. I was a lot stronger throughout all this than I thought I would be. I've had my days where I've cried myself to sleep with worry, not for him, but for those of us whom he left behind. There will always be that empty spot where he physically should be, but will only be in spirit and in memories.

I thank God for memories. It was truly the spirit of who Cotton was that is remembered. The shell that we saw and remember was just that; a shell. The essence of who Cotton was, was in the spirit of him. That's what I will hold onto forever. I smile, I laugh and I cry at the memories I hold dear. Our many summer vacation trips as a family, his high school graduation, his middle of the night calls to just chit chat, the nights of dragging me around town to karaoke spots so we could sing "Endless Love", a song we'd song at various weddings and other events, the first day my dad let him drive the car and he took me with him to pick up his paycheck and remembering the many dance contests he won when we were younger. I'm smiling now at the memories.

I woke up tonight at about 3:15am and was no longer sleepy. It's been over a month since we were once three, my two brothers and me. I wouldn't call this insomnia, but I had things on my mind that I needed to get off so I did some writing, hence this addition to my Saturday journal entry and to have a talk with my brother. I need to tell him I still miss him so much and that I'm doing alright. Brian and I took care of momma and daddy and we always will. We were once three, but now we're two, though we're still carrying the spirit of three.

December 2013 Journal Entry - God turned my pain into power. For months after Cotton passed I felt like a zombie without a purpose. I couldn't concentrate or focus because thoughts of how we were once three, my brothers and me and now we're two. Today, I still think of him each and every day, but God has made the endurance tolerable. I've turned my pain into power by deciding to sit down and write my first book. I didn't write a book about my brother, his life or the loss of him. I wrote what was in my heart at the time and that was romance. I did that because after three years I still needed an outlet for my frustration over missing my brother so much. I learned it doesn't matter what you write about, but that writing can be very therapeutic, so when you're down or in need of an outlet, put pen to paper and let it out.

I still journal and note thoughts I have about my brother, but I pour my heart and soul into writing novels, not because I'm a perfect writer, but because I love to tell a story and I find it makes everything in my life alright, including daily missing my brother.

Days still come up where I say to myself that we were once three, my brothers and me and now we're two carrying the spirit of three and it's alright now!

November 2014 - It feels wonderful sharing what was the hardest day of my life, the day my brother passed away. So much of what I want to do to inspire and encourage other's comes out of the peace God has given me that allows me to go on each day despite the hurt that comes along when I think that we were once three, my brothers and me and now we are two carrying the spirit of three and it's still alright!

~CARING~

God Cares
By Mary J. Demory

I was listening to the radio while driving home from work and I heard a radio personality tell a story as part of his daily spiritual encouragement segment. (10/22/14- Heaven 600 WCAO). He said he was driving past a school building and he noticed on the marquis in front that it had the letters "DOG RACES". He said he pondered why a school would be sponsoring dog races. He inquired of someone connected with the school about the dog races and they told him that it was not about dog races at all, it was to let people know that if they reversed the message it says "GOD CARES".

As I continued driving, by now almost home, I could not help but think about how much I know God cares and the many, many ways he shows me every second of my life that HE cares for me.

That evening and long into the next day it continued to resonate in my spirit how much God cares for me. I started reflecting on and reciting the instances that God showed up in my life and there was no dispute about how much He cared. The word of God says in 1 Peter 5:7 "God cares for you, so turn over all your worries to him; verse 10 says "He shows undeserved kindness to everyone". (Contemporary English version)

We have God's assurance that no matter the intensity of the problem He is with us and He cares. It would probably take too much time to try to name all of the situations where the storms of life come and it is only the knowledge of Our Heavenly Father's love and care that gets us through. When you reach the height of your frustration, when you are grieving, when someone you love walks out on you, when you are misunderstood or publicly humiliated, perhaps you have received a devastating diagnosis from your doctor or maybe you are totally confused about a decision or situation these are just a few of the circumstances where we feel His love.

God isn't looking for us to be perfect. He is patient, slow to anger and He is rich in grace and mercy. You should always anticipate that God will respond to you if you seek Him rather than allowing yourself to be burdened with anxiety or self-pity. Just trust that He loves you and He keeps His promises. Because of who God is and because of what God did by raising Jesus Christ from the dead, as Christians we have the assurance that there is hope because He Cares.

My mother had a quiet, determined spirit and she loved the Lord. When I would talk to her about a problem she always told me "trust God my child because God loves and cares for you." Her words and advice have stayed with me and that's why when I heard the radio personality talking about God Cares it took me back to my mother's wisdom and her sound advice because God has shown me more than enough that HE cares for me and I also know without a doubt that HE cares for you.

Respect God's care and rest in it.

~OVERCOMER~

Purpose From My Pain
By Wonda Oliver

Jabez was more honorable than his brothers. His mother had named him Jabez, saying, "I gave birth to him in pain." Jabez cried out to the God of Israel, "Oh that you would bless me and enlarge my territory! Let your hand be with me, and keep me from harm so that I will be free from pain." And God granted his request.   1Chronicles 4:9-10 (New International Version)

I sat in my home and reflected on the last few years of my life. I have been through so many major changes and I realized I was on the other side of many of my struggles. My mom passed away in my home on May 28, 2007. My daughter was five at the time and although I didn't think she fully understood what finding my mother like that meant, I later discovered it manifested itself in her fear of living in our house. Losing my mom was painful enough, but the thought that I would have to move and leave my house too, was horrific to me. On that day two years later I prayed and asked God to lead me and guide me. His answer to me was "Wait!", so I waited and I waited and while I waited I prayed and I prayed.

In case you don't know what God's voice sounds like, it's in the thoughts you have about making every decision you make. It is in the spirit of that person that smiles your way when you feel like no one cares. It is in the bible verse you read to get you up and out the door in the morning.

So as I continued along my journey and He continued to lead me and guide me, my daughter continued with her fear of the house. She would ask me every day, "mommy can we move or mommy when are we getting a new house?"

Through all of it I was still dealing with the pain of losing the best friend I had on earth, a father sick in a nursing home and a broken marriage.

Today I am here as a witness to you that as a result of my obedience to God, He has allowed me to see the full manifestation of His Glory! God made it so my godmother, one of my mom's closest and dearest friends needed a place to stay and she moved in with us. I witnessed my child not only go into my mom's room, but to get into the bed and fall asleep with my godmother just as she did with my mom in that very same room. Then she eventually said to me "mommy, I love our house".

I thought when I lost my mom and dad I would be all alone, but God has blessed me so that I have so much love surrounding me, peace that allows me to sleep at night and joy that makes me smile when I want to cry.

Please understand this, as hard as it may be, out of your pain God will bless you. It may seem rough now and you may not understand why you have to go through what you're going through, but God is able to do exceedingly abundantly and above all we can ask or think.

Jabez's mom named him because he brought her pain, but God set him apart from his brothers and when he cried out to the Lord, He heard him and granted his request. Don't look at your situation and say "Why Me?" Look at it and say,

"Thank you God for choosing me." Believe that if He picked you, He knew you could handle it. He chose you and when you call to Him, He knows your voice and He will answer your request. When He blesses you, watch out because He's going to bless you with Greater!

I encourage you today to look back at some of your painful moments and see what blessings have come as a result of that pain. Don't look for the material, although that may be how God blessed you, but look at the peace you have now, the joy he has filled you with, and the love that surrounds you.

~BLESSED~

Our "Littles"
By LaTonya Summerville

It was October 15, 2010 and I can't help but to think if what I had done on January 5, 2010 had led to this; the most devastating day thus far if my adult life.

My husband and I had plans of having a double date with my sister-in-law and her date. We were going to go see a movie and have dinner, we had planned to meet up with them after our doctor's appointment. Instead we ended up in the hospital. I had a hand full of tissues that were soaked with my tears and the other hand was shaking while I handed my insurance card to the nice Indian woman at the registration desk. She told me don't cry, everything will be alright.

What we had announced to our family over a spaghetti dinner at our home, life, ended with the stop of his heartbeat. Why?

As I laid in the hospital room, I wondered why I had to hear for the second time that there is no heartbeat. What did they mean, no heartbeat? We were just playing and reading Humpty Dumpty together. Why?

We just wrote out over 100 invitations to our baby shower. We registered for our baby's gifts. We were excited about if our baby was going to be a girl or a boy? We called the baby "Littles" the entire time I carried him; 29 weeks in my womb. He went to work with me, he heard me laugh and he felt my cry. No one else knew me like he did. Why?

No one told me that I could lose my baby at such an advance stage in my pregnancy. What I knew is that the first six weeks of pregnancy was the 'critical' stage and after that it was fine and safe to announce to the world that we were expecting. Why?

Why did God take my baby that he gave me? Littles was a surprise; he was not planned but OH BOY we were super excited to hear of the news that he was conceived. The glow my husband and I had was undeniably golden. We had plans to have children and we were, but I had made the decision to be a healthier me and have weight loss surgery, so I did. While I was on my journey to becoming healthy, that is when Littles decided to join us. We decided early on to call the baby Littles because our dear friend would always ask, how is Littles because no one knew if he was a girl or boy.

Back to that day, October 15, we left the hospital to tell the news to our parents that Littles heart had stopped beating and returned to the hospital the next day. On October 16, 2010 I had to have my labor induced and 18 hours later on October 17, 2010, Littles arrived and it was true, his heart was not beating.

With the love and support of our Pastor, family and friends, we had a graveside funeral and buried our angel baby at a cemetery that has a Children's Garden. It was important that we gave Littles a respectful send off because God gave us him and whatever God trusts you with, especially life, you cherish and take care of it. We were devastated for our loss, yet appreciative for the 29 weeks we got to spend together as a family.

Ladies, the minute you find out that you are pregnant, go set up appointments with an OBGYN/Obstetrician. Pay close attention to your body, the suspicious signs and the baby's activity patterns. Never put off or procrastinate to seek medical care. I did all of the right things and unfortunately my pregnancy ended with a loss. It was tragic, but God graced us with the peace and strength to get through it all.

We celebrate Littles' birthday and it is a family holiday. My husband and I take off of work and along with our baby girl Lyric, we hang out together and visit his grave site.

Lyric was born a year after Littles. We promised Littles that we would keep his memory alive and tell his siblings that come after him all about him. He was our first, our oldest and our most triumphant achievement. We have a slogan in his memory "Smile For Littles".

There are support groups for families that have similar experiences, so reach out if you need to talk. Don't go through something like this alone.

~STAND~

God is in Control
By Irishteen Thomas

Life can deal many kinds of blows. Some of them are expected, some are not. We live in a world that has many trials and tribulations. If we are to survive, we must press forward and stay strong. Know that you are not alone. It is not always easy to come out of the doldrums; but come out you must. Setbacks can make or break you. One thing that we must know and remember is that behind every cloud there is a silver lining. With that thought in mind, there is hope. Hope that you can and will overcome, hope that there is a brighter side somewhere.

This is to a sister who has almost lost hope. Keep in mind that the word 'Almost' means that you are still standing. You have not hit rock bottom yet and trust me you will not hit rock bottom as long as God is in charge. Know it, embrace it and rest in the fact that He is working for you. Fight through this season and stay faithful to God.

This is to a sister who believes that the enemy has you where he wants you. Wake up sister and know that if a door has closed for you another one will open. Many times, doors close because when and if we walk through, we will be walking where God does not want us at the time. Remember, He has a plan for your life. What God has for you, it is for you. Wait on it, anticipate it.

Let me encourage you to not give up. Read your Word, pray without ceasing and try to see a bit of good in all that you encounter. I believe that you have the ability to become a walking, talking, praising miracle. Set your mind on the things that your master and only your master is able to do.

Remember, we serve a good and merciful God who loves His children. Try not to walk alone. Surround yourself with believers who will walk with you. You will make it. Stay strong my sister and be blessed! Remember who is in control.

~UNDERSTANDING~

Compassion Flowing From My Heart to Your Heart
By Dr. Simone P. Gibson

The essence of sisterhood flows from close relationships among women fostered through shared experiences and concerns. It is through our sisterhood that we are able to help one another by providing strength, courage, resource and resolve. There is a well-known bible story that speaks to the heart of sisterhood…"Compassion flowing from heart to heart".

Webster dictionary defines compassion as a 'sympathetic consciousness of others' distress together with a desire to alleviate it." Oftentimes when we think of compassion in the Bible we consider that scriptures will often say that Jesus was moved with compassion before He healed, delivered or helped someone in need. The parable Jesus told about the Good Samaritan in St. Luke, Chapter 10 speaks profoundly about compassion and shows how it flows from heart to heart. This flow of consideration, empathy and kindness engenders sisterhood.

The Good Samaritan is an excellent example for us on why compassion is important. The story is a familiar one where a man is robbed and left for dead and a priest and a Levite cross over to the other side rather than stopping to help him, while a Samaritan not only assists him in his needs, but also makes provisions for his recovery. The focus in this parable is usually on the actions of the Good Samaritan, but I want us to consider the thoughts that may have led him to take action. This is an important part of this story.

It would appear that something moved within the heart of the Samaritan, drawing him outside of himself to extend himself to someone else. The history of the Samaritan people is a troubled one; they were considered outcasts, immoral people without heritage and culture. Their race was despised and looked at as inferior by the Jews of Biblical times. One could infer that perhaps this Samaritan was someone who although was successful, had been rejected, perhaps even pushed aside. He probably had experienced much pain and hurt in his life. The compassion that emerged from the heart of the Samaritan to the heart of this man, who was badly wounded, probably materialized from a heart that had experienced deep wounds itself. He understood what it felt like to be hurt, rejected and abused and perhaps knew what it felt like for others to cross over to the other side, rather than deal with him. Compassion flowed from his heart to the heart of this hurting man.

The lesson for us sisters is we should not close ourselves to compassion and the ministry that God will allow to flow from our hearts. Oftentimes because of our circumstances, the pain, rejection and suffering that we have or are enduring, we close our hearts and will not allow compassion to flow. The enemy of our souls would like to keep us buried in our pain and suffering. He does not want us to release the fragrance of mercy and grace to help a sister in need. The enemy wants to isolate us into thinking that it's only me, I am the only one who is going through or have gone through this and I have nothing to give anyone else.

Our greatest challenge is to allow the Holy Spirit to cause

us to rise above our own circumstances and reach out to a sister who is in need. Perhaps that sister has experienced the same things that you have experienced and because of your personal experiences, you can minster love and support. Sisters let us rise up and soar above our current state and allow the Spirit of compassion to emerge from our hearts and flow into another sister's heart solidifying the great gift of Sisterhood. Let us testify to one another that God is more for us than the world against us....I made it through and so will you!

~INFLUENCE~

I Can, You Can
By Susie D. Lang

In October 2014, I walked the 5k Race for the Cure to raise much needed funds for research to find a cure for breast cancer. Being a six year survivor, I was still amazed at the thousands of female and male survivors who either walked or raced for the same cause.

When I first found out I had breast cancer, my only thought was how do I tell my family and how will they respond. Personally, for me I was fine. I knew twenty years prior, breast cancer could have been the cause of my death. However, in 2007 I knew that only three percent of women were dying from breast cancer and I would not be one of them. God and I had already had our conversation about this. My family took it very well. They were extremely supportive of me as was the staff at Greater Baltimore Medical Breast Cancer Center. I said to the surgeon "do what you have to do; I have places to go, people to see and things to do." I was not concerned about people knowing. I wanted them to know because I firmly believe that accepting an illness and moving on with your life is half the battle. I love life and I want to live as long as I can.

Therefore, on January 10, 2008 I underwent surgery on my left breast and reconstruction on both. To this day, I have never regretted the decision I made. The surgery was a breeze. The radiation treatment and the horrendous burning of my skin as a result nearly sent me into a spin of depression. Nevertheless, I was determined to be victorious through all of this, and I was! Thank you Lord!

In 2012, a thirty-seven year old relative was diagnosed with breast cancer. Other than me, we have no history of breast cancer in the family. Naturally, I was there to encourage her and push her on. No need because like me, she knew we serve a GOOD GOD who had this in control.

In 2013 she underwent a mastectomy on her left breast. My recuperation was no less than eight months. This champion was out of the hospital and on her feet within three months. I say it again 'Ain't GOD GOOD!' Today, that relative is doing great and studying to further her career.

I am reminded what the songwriter wrote "as I look back over my life and I think things over I can truly say that I've been blessed I've got a testimony."

Be blessed my sister for no matter what life sends our way, know that we were born to overcome life's obstacles and destined to be victorious if we remember who we are and whose we are.

Special thanks to my good friend, Ms. Carol V. Dorsey for being right there through all of it. I love you.

~Hope~

Try Again
By Cheryl Barton

Misery loves company, or so you think
The ship is going down, do you get off or just sink.
Life throws you a curveball, you may want to run
Why not stick around, your best is yet to come.

Some paths seem dark, many have no light
Don't give up thinking no good is in sight.
Things may seem bleak every now and then,
Dust yourself off, stand and try again.

I've had my own share of being up then down
I know how quickly a smile can turn into a frown.
I thought about life and how sad it would be
If I didn't let go of the heartache, just set it free.

I know you've heard it before, I'm preaching to the choir
But making sure you never give up, I'll never tire.
I have no doubt that when you get to that great end
You'll say it was well worth trying again.

~TOUCH~

What's For Me?
By Michelle Russell

I met a woman walking today,
She seemed much less able than me.
A winter coat this day in June,
I thought all her belongings to be.

Had she worn it long all her life?
Is it her something after nothing?
Has she touched someone significantly?
Is her fortune gone or coming?

Just at the beginning of summer,
This evening turned windy and cold.
I pull a thick wooly sweater,
Subtracting the nip from the cold.

I feel the winds sound a change,
I wonder what's in it for me.
Will I wear this thick wooly sweater?
Will I have touched significantly?

Contributors

Cheryl Barton

Cheryl Barton is an author who was born and raised in Baltimore, Maryland, where she works full-time and writes novels.

As a romance novelist, Cheryl released her first novel, 'Bachelor Not for Sale' in April 2013. Following this release, she has authored nine additional novels, including two follow-ups to 'Bachelor Not for Sale', 'A Designed Affair' and 'A Perfect Combination'. She also released 'The Artist', 'The Bookkeeper', 'The Chef' and 'The Dancer', the first four in a new twenty-six, Amorous Occupations book series. She also released a holiday short story, 'Holly for Christmas', a Valentine Novella, 'Second Chances' and combining romance with inspiration, she released 'Down, But Not Out: Breaking Chains' in mid-2014. For more information on these and upcoming novels, visit her website at www.cherylbarton.net.

Cheryl is the owner of Barton Publishing, LLC, a media publishing company and is excited about book projects from new writers under her publishing label. Visit the publishing company website at www.bartonpublishingLLC.com.

Cheryl is the Founder and Executive Director of Sisters About Making Moves, Inc., (SAMM) a non-profit organization whose mission is to educate, embrace and empower sisterhood within the community. This organization has championed a toiletry drive for the House of Ruth of Maryland and for the city's homeless community through its Blessing Bags giveaway.

Cheryl is a member of the Black Writers' Guild of Maryland and is the proud mother of one daughter, Chynae Victoria.

Barbara Barton

Barbara Barton is a retiree of Verizon who loves spending time with family. She has been married to John, the love of her life for 51 years and she is the mother of three, grandmother of six, great-grandmother of seven and a surrogate mother to many.

Chynae V. Barton

Chynae was born and raised in Baltimore, Maryland. She is an undergraduate student at Morgan State University seeking a Bachelor's degree in the School of Social Work.

In the summer of 2014, she was an intern working for Baltimore's city council president. The experience helped her gain important social skills and advanced technical skills that she'll need in order to be successful in her future field of work.

Kimberly P. Carter

Kim has been a Registered Nurse for over 21 years. She holds a Bachelor's Degree in Nursing and a Master's of Science Degree in Nursing Education.

Kim is a member of Tau Eta Zeta Chapter of Zeta Phi Beta Sorority, Inc., in Baltimore, Maryland. She serves as the chapter's Elections Chair, a member of the Membership Committee and she serves on the Board of the Sharon K. Harvey Memorial Foundation.

Kim is the proud mother of one son. She's an Independent Consultant with Thirty-One Gifts, one of the leading direct sales companies in the US. www.mythirtyone.com/127393

Mary J. Demory

Mary J. Demory a native Baltimorean, Christian, Social Worker by training, community leader and church leader has dedicated much of her life to initiatives and organizations that impact women's issues, their achievements as well as their problems. As a seasoned leader, she is a role-model and an encourager. She believes that more women should use their God given gifts to achieve their dreams and to feel empowered.

Sandra L. Fletcher

Sandra L. Fletcher was an Information Systems professional with the Social Security Administration, where she retired after 30 years of federal service. Since retirement, she invests much of her time working in ministry, primarily at her home church, Kingdom Light Ministries where she is the Director of Finance and functions in many other areas of ministry including serving on the Board of Trustees and instructing their New Members Classes. She is also a Tax Preparer and is the proprietor of Fletcher's Financial Services.

Sandra was married to Johnnie Fletcher, Sr., for 45 years at the time of his death. She is the mother of two children and one grandson. She values her special relationship with her son's fiancé and her grandson's wife. Sandra is the proud great-grandmother of 3 girls.

Her most notable achievement is being a child of God. Sandi is currently pursuing coursework at Redeemed International Christian College. She is a licensed Minister and aims to teach the word of God with simplicity and practicality.

Dr. Simone Gibson

Dr. Simone Gibson was born in the beautiful island of Jamaica, West Indies. She accepted Jesus Christ as her personal savior while watching a television broadcast in Jamaica and rededicated her life to the Lord and was baptized during her junior year in college. The Lord has filled her with His Spirit and her constant prayer is that He will continue to fill her cup so that it will overflow. Believing in the importance of higher education and with the support of her family, Dr. Gibson has furthered her education. She has received a Bachelor's Degree in Chemistry from the University of Maryland Baltimore County (UMBC), a Master's Degree in Spiritual & Pastoral Care from Loyola College in Baltimore and the Doctor of Ministry Degree from United Theological Seminary in Dayton, Ohio with concentration in Preaching and Leadership.

She has served for over 17 years at the Transformation Church of Jesus Christ first as the Executive Administrator. Her assignment now is to serve as the Executive Assistant to Bishop Monroe Saunders, Jr., D.Min., (Pastor of Transformation Church and Presiding Prelate of the United Church of Jesus Christ). An ordained elder in the United Church of Jesus Christ, Dr. Gibson has been a faithful member of the Transformation Church as well as the United Church of Jesus Christ serving in a variety of ministries over the years.

Dr. Gibson is the President and CEO of Run Tell It Ministries, LLC, a ministry purposed to equip and empower lives to show forth HIS Glory. Run Tell It Ministries has facilitated a mentorship program for young women. In addition the ministry hosted for two years the "Because of Who You are Conference." Dr. Gibson has been married to Elder Daniel Gibson for over 20 years. Her greatest desire is "to shew forth the praises of Him who hath called her out of darkness into His marvelous light", to reveal God's glory in all that she says and do and to be a blessing to His people".

Teresa Graves

Teresa D. Graves was born and raised in Baltimore, Maryland. She is a twenty-five year employee with the State of Maryland. She is the mother of two and the MaTee (grandmother) of Miles, Sanaya and Khalil.

In her spare time, she enjoys reading, writing poems, watching the Baltimore Ravens, bowling, eating steamed crabs and traveling.

Teresa is also a member of Sisters About Making Moves (SAMM) a community service organization and the owner of Handbags and More.

Susie D. Lang

Susie is a wife, mother, grandmother and great-grandmother. She is a retiree of the C&P Telephone Company and is currently employed as a Staff Associate for the City of Baltimore, Office of the City Council President Bernard C. "Jack" Young.

Susie loves to sing, shop, travel and serve God to the best of her ability as a longtime member of the United Baptist Church.

Her two best girlfriends of 55 years are Mary A. Alston of Baltimore, Maryland and Vanita C. Green of Roxboro, North Carolina. "To God be the Glory!"

Jaye Matthews

Jaye Matthews, CEO of J. Matthews International, L.L.C., is quite the contender in Marketing/PR Strategies & Innovation. With over eighteen years of experience, Jaye launched & operated her very first company, J-Spot Marketing & Promotions, from her dorm room in 1996 while still an undergraduate college student. Jaye, a current DBA Candidate, is now equipped with relevant experience in the Marketing, Public Relations & Multimedia industries and is often referred to as "The Marketing & Media Maven." Having worked in Operations for the International sector and in Talent Coordination & Production for a major cable television network, as well as being a nationally recognized & respected on-air Media Personality, Jaye is more than capable of bringing relevance to merely existing businesses, causes, events, individuals, organizations, products and services, globally.

Jaye resides in Baltimore, Maryland, serves as a Licensed Minister at the Transformation Church of Jesus Christ – Apostolic and is an Adjunct Professor in the area of Communications at various colleges. She loves children and has established a charity called Toasty Tots Movement which provides kids up to age five with brand new coats in an effort to give them a hug of warmth to last all winter long.

www.JayeMatthews.com
Twitter: @StrateJaye

Mia Minion

Mia was born in Washington, D.C. but has lived in Baltimore most of her life. Mia has one son and two grandchildren. She has been a member of Set the Captives Free Outreach Center (STCFOC) since 2006. She graduated from Northwestern High School in 1978 and went on to complete her Bachelor's Degree in Management Science from Coppin State University in 1985. She has been working for the Federal Government for twenty-nine years and is now attending Walden University where she is actively pursuing her Master's Degree in Communications.

Geezie Reaves

Gwenaviere (Geezie) Reaves was born in Lans de Bu Sac, France, a military brat, but was raised from childhood right here in Baltimore City. At any early age, she realized the importance of encouragement through family. As a child she enjoyed writing in and on everything she touched. As we know life can deal some heavy blows, she endured much pain growing up which helped to strengthen her faith.

Geezie is a loving daughter, proud mother and braggadocios grandmother. She has always used encouraging words to strengthen and guide her sons.

She has worked for the state of Maryland for fourteen years and is into her second career. In addition to working, she is attending the University of Baltimore pursuing her Bachelor of Science degree in Criminal Justice. She feels a strong desire to touch other's lives, so she is currently working on a Daily Inspirational Blog that she posts faithfully to every day. She also has her own page on Facebook titled "A Praying Woman of God". Her passion for writing has finally raised and the opportunity has been offered through this new unique book project; One Sister Away. This is a great beginning to her heartfelt dream to write her own inspirational book. She is so proud to be a part of this exciting venture. Her desire to inspire other sisters is being released whole heartedly through this project. You can enjoy her collection of prayers and inspirational messages on her daily blog at http://gz4life.blogspot.com/

Michelle Russell

Born and raised in Baltimore MD, Michelle has been writing poetry and short stories as a hobby since childhood. Her writing has compelling, transitional phrases that take the reader from imagination to realistic and memorable moments. She is mother of three very talented and very different young men.

Michelle also enjoys a very real and very loving relationship with a true ride or die brother, her lover and friend for over eleven years.

Michelle gave her life to Christ as an adult in May of 2001. She uses her Human Resources and Accounting background, right and left brain, to manage an awesome group of payroll professionals at a Maryland born and bred Christian owned corporation.

Laniece Oliver

Laniece Oliver is a twelve year old seventh grade student at the Maryland School for the Deaf. She is the founder of the Miss Deaf Dream America organization, whose mission is to encourage and empower other young Deaf and Hard of Hearing girls so that they know that anything is possible.

Laniece is the 2012 Miss Maryland Sweetheart for the Miss American Coed Pageants and the 2013 Miss District of Columbia United States Preteen. Laniece is a staff model with the J and Company Christian Models Inc. and a member of the 2015 team USA for the World Championship of Performing Arts.

Laniece believes "Whatever you decide to do, make sure it makes you happy.

Wonda Oliver

Wonda Oliver is a woman walking in God's will in order to be a living manifestation of his power. She is looking forward, not backward and praising God each step of the way.

Wonda is the founder and owner of Oliver Event Planners (OEP), a social event and lifestyle management company. OEP's mission is to help people realize and reach their full potential. She is also a proud mom of one daughter Laniece and God mom of six.

Latonya Summerville

LaTonya Summerville considers herself one of the luckiest wives, mother, daughter and friend around! Currently she is a Legal Studies student pursuing her Bachelor of Science Degree at the University of Maryland, University College with a minor in Healthcare Administration. She is in the business of Medical Billing and Coding and she has an Associate of Arts Degree and a Certified Professional Coding Certificate. She works as a Coding Quality Auditor and an Adjunct Faculty Member. LaTonya is also a Mary Kay Consultant and can be reached at http://www.marykay.com/lsummerville.

Besides family time her favorite past time hobbies are glam sessions, shopping sprees, baking, coding and helping and supporting others. Her dream is to one day host her own talk show titled Tea Thyme With La.

Kaylani Thomas

Kaylani Thomas is a fourth grade student who loves pets, especially cats, karate, riding her bike and watching old Shirley Temple movies. Her favorite food is pepperoni pizza and when she grows up she wants to be a writer like her dad.

Irishteen Thomas

Irishteen Thomas attended Booker T. Washington, Douglass High School, and Coppin State University, graduating with a Bachelor's Degree in Elementary Education. She also attended Baltimore City Community College in order to renew her certification in reading. She was employed by the Baltimore City School System for 32 rewarding and gratifying years.

Presently, she is a Baltimore City Public School substitute teacher. Her hobbies include reading, working with children, shopping and working for the Lord. Her immediate family includes a daughter, son, granddaughter and a great grandson, who is the apple of her eye.

Irishteen hopes that she is able to lift someone's spirit through her words of encouragement.

About Barton Publishing, LLC

Barton Publishing, LLC is a company dedicated to helping writers become authors. Our foundation is based on the belief that there is a writer in all of us just waiting to be birthed. Get moving toward that dream today!

Our company motto is, "Your Dreams Are Safe in Our Hands" and we stand behind that.

For more information on the services provided by Barton Publishing, visit our website at www.bartonpublishingLLC.com

www.ingramcontent.com/pod-product-compliance
Lightning Source LLC
Chambersburg PA
CBHW051806040426
42446CB00007B/542